I WISH I WAS

For Valerie,

Every Blessing

Anona.

I WISH I WAS

A true story of fear and rejection, hope and redemption

Anona Coates

Authentic

MILTON KEYNES ● COLORADO SPRINGS ● HYDERABAD

This edition published 2008 by Authentic Media
9 Holdom Avenue, Bletchley, Milton Keynes, MK1 1QR, UK
1820 Jet Stream Drive, Colorado Springs, CO 80921, USA
OM Authentic Media, Medchal Road, Jeedimetla Village,
Secunderabad 500 055, A.P., India
www.authenticmedia.co.uk

Authentic Media is a division of IBS-STL U.K., limited by guarantee, with its
Registered Office at Kingstown Broadway, Carlisle, Cumbria CA3 0HA.
Registered in England & Wales No. 1216232. Registered charity 270162

British Library Cataloguing in Publication Data
A catalogue record for this book is available from the British Library

ISBN-13: 978-1-86024-701-9

Cover Design by Andy Newbold
Print Management by Adare
Printed in Great Britain by J.H. Haynes & Co., Sparkford

For Gerald, my best friend

Contents

Acknowledgements

My husband Gerald and my three sons Paul, Simon and Jonathan have been the most precious people in my life. I once said to the boys, 'When you are grown up we may not agree on everything, but we must stay friends, and we have. Thank you, I love you. Loving thanks also to my sister Kathryn Green, and my brothers Vic Ayling and Nick Edge. You have been gracious enough to allow me to tell your story as well as my own.

So many friends, too numerous to mention by name – you know who you are – encouraged me to write this book. Thank you, I hope you enjoy it. Two friends in particular have made it possible. Amanda Williams was faithful enough to phone me one day and tell me something that changed my life. Everlasting thanks, Amanda. Robyn Blood not only patiently typed out the first few drafts of the manuscript, but encouraged me greatly as I dug up my past. Bless you, Robyn.

Malcolm Down from Authentic believed, as I did, that others who had gone through similar experiences to me could be helped by reading my story. Thank you for your faith in me. My editor, Sheila Jacobs, has done an amazing job in drawing out the heart of the book and making it so accessible. It has been wonderful to work with you.

Introduction

One day, when I was forty-three years of age, I found a skeleton in my cupboard. The amazing thing was, it looked just like me.

As I stared at my mirror image, I wondered, 'Who is she? Where has she come from?' Identical in appearance, she was a normal, middle-aged woman but she was known by another name. She had a different identity, a different family, people knew about her . . . but I'd had no idea that she even existed. She had a past I knew nothing about, but a future that would be changed by what I'd discovered. I knew for sure, from that day on, my life would never be the same.

To be at peace with myself I had to find out about her. I took a deep breath, stepped into the cupboard and we merged into one.

1

Remembering

I had no idea that the next few minutes would change my life forever.

The sun was shining and all was well with the world. I parked the car and walked into my house. The phone was ringing and I answered it.

'Hello! Anona speaking.'

'Hi,' said a familiar voice. 'Amanda here.'

I had only just left Amanda's house. It was the day I regularly set aside for taking my elderly mother out for a drive. We had done some shopping at a local garden centre, eaten lunch there and then called in at Amanda's house for a cup of tea.

'I must tell you,' said Amanda, 'that woman is not your mother!'

'Well,' I replied, taken aback by her adamant tone, 'I know we don't look alike. She's shorter and was dark-haired. But I take after my father. He was taller and fairer—'

'No!' replied Amanda, firmly. 'It's not just appearances. There's *nothing* similar about you.'

I collapsed into a chair, my mind spinning. And instead of immediately dismissing her words, the thought came into my head: 'Perhaps she's right.'

At forty-three, I had a good life by anyone's standards. I was happily married, and had three healthy sons, two old enough to leave the nest. Paul, the eldest, had already left home and was renting a cottage with a friend. Although not wealthy, we were comfortably off financially and were fortunate to live in an historic house in the Surrey town of Esher. We had bought it a few years before with another married couple, Norman Miller and Sheila Walsh, who spent most of the year in America and were happy for us to decorate and look after it as we liked. I enjoyed my part-time job as a doctor's receptionist and was fortunate to have many good friends.

I had not thought about my early years for a long time. Life was full and satisfying – but there were some niggling doubts.

Like many children, I had always thought I was the 'odd one out'. My family were country people who enjoyed gardening and animals. I had hated my clothes being covered in dog hairs and craved culture and elegance, even though I had no idea what that really meant. And then, of course, there was Dad . . .

Over the next couple of weeks, I began to remember the years I had tried to forget.

Growing up in the English countryside in the 1950s should have been such fun. I lived in a village called Effingham in the county of Surrey; it was very much open country at that time.

Parents did not seem to have any fears for their children's safety. My friends and I would leave home after breakfast, clutching brown paper bags containing sandwiches, apples and sultanas. If we felt thirsty, we would knock on the door of the nearest house and ask for a drink of water.

Our journey would take us to the top of our road and into the woodland. There, our dreams could be acted out. In my imagination I would be a princess, very beautiful and benevolent, adored by my subjects. I was sure that I had some royal connection as my surname was Ayling, meaning 'Of noble and royal blood'. Each tree would be judged for its suitability as a palace, a house, a school or a hospital. Even thick hedges could be utilised. We would not even need any props, perhaps an old rag as a curtain or a rusty tin plate. Our imagination would provide the rest.

We considered ourselves invisible to adults and would be surprised if an irate farmer ordered us off his land. Everyone writes about bluebells in their memoirs, but I really do remember the beautiful carpets of bluebells with the sunlight shining through the beech trees above.

There were a few odd people around but we would know to keep out of their way. Even our resident tramp, Wurzel Gummidge, seemed no threat to us. Rumour had it that he came from a wealthy background but had chosen a different way of life. He lived in a hut in the woods and would often be found knocking on doors asking, 'Have you a cup of tea spare, missus?'

I lived in Woodlands Road. At the bottom was the main road going from Leatherhead to Guildford. My friends and I would take a notebook and sit on the kerb, writing down the number plates of passing cars. We had plenty of time to do this as not many cars went by. They were nearly all black so we made a special note of a maroon or (my favourite) a dark green one when it appeared. Here also were the bus stops for the 408 route. I spent a huge amount of my early years standing at those bus stops counting to 100, then 200, hoping and praying that a bus would come into view soon.

When I was quite small, I was apparently very bold. At about three years of age I had left the house, walked quite a distance down the road and was about to board the bus when a neighbour recognised me and took me home. I'd had a penny in my pocket and said I was going shopping. My mother told me later that when I was little I had no fear: 'You walked out into the world, expecting it to be kind to you.' Most of the time, it was. I would often wander off, knock on people's doors and be invited in. I once reckoned I had visited every house in our road. And yet, by the time I was fifteen, I'd no longer be the bold and fearless child I had been when young. I was painfully shy with no self-confidence and no idea of what the future would hold.

Examining my past, I can see just how this happened – and why. All the clues were there, I just didn't see them at the time.

2

Early Days

Until I was four years old, life was an adventure. After the shortages during the war, mothers were proud to have fat babies – they spoke of health and prosperity – and I certainly was one. My only defect was that my ears stuck out. Mum tried to remedy this by sticking them back with Sellotape, but it didn't work. Still, I even came second in a 'Beautiful Baby' competition so I must have been quite appealing, with my curly blonde hair and cheeky grin.

Although I had some toys to play with, I really enjoyed following Mum around the house, 'helping'. I blame my dislike of cooking on an accident I had when I was tiny – Mum was baking cakes and I was kneeling on a high stool, when I slipped, fell to the floor and chipped my elbow. Apparently my arm was in a sling for two weeks but I was 'very good about it'. (My excuse now, when I pop a frozen meal into the microwave, is 'I associate cooking with pain'!)

Very few mothers went out to work just after the war, but they had plenty to do in their homes, which had no modern conveniences. Regardless of the weather, each day was set. Monday was washday, not my favourite. Mum would pull out the big metal boiler, light the gas under it and stir the washing in the hot water. It would then be rinsed and wrung out through the mangle or wringer. You had to be very careful not to catch your fingers between the rollers. If the weather was fine, the clothes could be hung on the line that stretched down the length of the garden but if not, they had to be draped on a wooden clothes horse in front of the fire, steaming for the rest of the day. Because washing was such a chore, everyone made their clothes last as long as possible – even underwear was worn for a whole week. Tuesday was ironing day. Mum used old-fashioned flat irons heated on the gas hob – very difficult to regulate the temperature. Dusting and polishing were my favourites on Wednesdays. Thursdays or Fridays we would go on the bus to the nearby village of Great Bookham for the shopping which could not be bought at the corner shop or delivered. Outside the newsagents in the high street was a giant ice cream cone, about three feet tall. One day, coming out of the shop in a daydream, I walked straight into it and knocked myself out.

Great Bookham was also the scene of my first alcoholic drink. Mum and Dad had made one of their rare visits to a pub, The Royal Oak, and I was left outside in my large maroon and cream pram. Apparently I screamed and screamed and could only be placated by sipping beer from a glass.

During this time, Dad's parents, who lived in a bungalow only a road away, began to have health problems and needed a lot of attention. Most of the work was left to Mum. Many years later, she related how a neighbour would knock on the door and tell her a doctor had called on the grandparents and a prescription was needed.

She told me this: 'I would strap you into your pram with some toys and leave you in the kitchen, go to the bus stop, catch the bus to Bookham, collect the medicine, take it to the "old ones" and, do you know what? When I arrived home, I found you had thrown out all of your toys.'

I worked out that journey would have taken about two hours.

We lived in a detached house with three bedrooms, two double and a box room. Downstairs there was a front room, furnished with old heavy furniture and an aspidistra plant in the window. I only remember this room in use with the fire lit on Christmas Day and Boxing Day. The back room was the kitchen. This was our living room where we ate our meals and sat on the straight-backed dining chairs reading in the evenings. The actual kitchen was called a scullery and later, Dad added the bathroom. As a small child, I did not have a bedroom. For quite a while, I slept on an old army camp bed on the landing. A hole appeared in the khaki canvas and, each night, I was petrified that it would give way and I would drop six inches to the floor. Then when Granny, my mum's mother, moved in with us, I shared her bed. Although Granny was immaculately clean I can still remember the smell of decay that surrounds an old person's body. One day, Mum heard that it was not good for a child to sleep with an old person, so a bed was acquired for me and I moved into the box room. It certainly lived up to its name. Dad was a carpenter and used it as a storeroom for his two large tool chests. These were covered with old curtain material, and served as the only furniture, other than a bed. On the wall hung a glass case with stuffed birds and animals, enough to give nightmares to a small child.

As I grew older, I tried to make the room more homely. A high corner shelf held my books, with clothes hanging from hooks underneath. Propped up amongst my clothes were Dad's three shotguns – not loaded. All my other possessions were in a suitcase under the bed. Perhaps, from this, I should have realised that my parents thought my stay might only be temporary.

For most of my childhood, we had no electricity in the house, just gas; you had to be very careful when lighting the gas mantles so as not to puncture them. It was rather like living in Victorian times. Until electricity was connected, I would go to bed with a torch, great for reading under the covers. I was always sent to bed really early and would lay awake for two or three hours, feeling very lonely. Like most working-class people, we had no central heating so in winter we would wear more clothes in bed than we wore during the day. Cardigans were worn on top of winceyette nighties, and we had bed socks so our feet could rest on a hot-water bottle without getting too many chilblains. In the morning I would trace with my finger the wonderful patterns of ice on the inside of the windows; Jack Frost had called.

My parents never owned a car, never flew in a plane or even travelled any great distance. Bicycles, buses and trains were our mode of transport and, from an early age, I was determined to try them all. My father had a distrust of anything modern. 'That infernal combustion engine!' he would roar when motors were mentioned. He was, however, happy to accept a lift in a car.

Other than clothes bought twice yearly, spring and autumn, in Leatherhead or Guildford, all our shopping was done locally. A few doors away from our house were two corner shops. One sold groceries, tinned food, fruit and vegetables. I was born in 1947 so rationing was still in place. Food was in short supply and very expensive; it could cost up to 70 per cent of a working man's weekly wage. I can remember Mum and me walking to the shops with our ration books. Mum would ask for the items she needed for that day; we didn't have a refrigerator so everything was fresh. Self-service had not been invented – the shopkeeper would have been horrified if a customer had tried to do her job by picking up the groceries. A short chat about the weather and Mrs Jones' corns, and our shopping trip was complete. But what about the sweets? Well, when I was very little there were none; Mum would sometimes make me sugar sandwiches with white bread and white sugar. But a few years later, I was able to feed my sweet tooth with a bag of sweets chosen from huge glass jars. Heaven!

Many household items were delivered to the door: coal for the open fire – our only form of heating for many years – bread, newspapers and, my favourite, milk. This was delivered by horse and cart and if we were lucky the horse would choose the spot outside our house to do its business and Mum would rush out with a shovel. Ideal manure for the garden!

'Can I have a ride, mister?' I'd ask.

'All right, young 'un.'

I would stand at the front of the cart with the reins in my hand, feeling like a charioteer as the poor horse trudged its way up the hill.

We were quite self-sufficient with a long narrow garden, flowers in the front and vegetables in the back. We also kept chickens and ducks so eggs were always available. I don't remember us eating the chickens – they were probably too tough – but we certainly ate the rabbits Mum bred. It did seem a little strange to be sitting at the table eating Fluffy, the rabbit I'd been playing with the day before.

Meals were very important at our house. We had a good breakfast, and dinner was the main meal, eaten at lunchtime – always meat and two veg with a pudding – then tea at 6 p.m. with sandwiches and cake. This changed in later years when Dad was at work further away; then, we ate our main meal at 6 p.m. but it was still called tea.

Very few luxuries were available in the early years after the Second World War; no one had snacks between meals so our stomachs were always rumbling by the time we ate. Mum hated cooking; she said she longed for the day when we could just take a tablet – everything took so long. She would start to prepare a meal two hours before, home-made pies, steamed puddings and stews, all from fresh ingredients. Our family meal times should have been enjoyable after all that work and the best of ingredients, but they were times of purgatory. Mum always had the pressure of getting the food to the table 'on the dot' and we ate in silence unless Dad wanted to say something. If a pea slid off my plate onto the floor that would warrant a 'clip around the ear', which sounds harmless but was, in fact, a whack around the head with the back of Dad's hand.

But in spite of all this, my very early years were not unhappy. Then, just before my fourth birthday my life began to change.

3

Living with Dad

The day that marked the turning point is still clear in my mind. I walked over to my mother to sit on her lap for a cuddle and she pushed me away.

'You're too big for that now,' she said.

I was devastated. It was as if something inside me died that day. My sense of rejection was so great; I felt hurt and alone and thought, 'I will never do that again.'

Many years later, I asked Mum why she had responded like that. She shrugged and replied, 'Dad told me not to show you any more affection.'

The next life-changing event was on one cold March morning. I was sitting on the floor under the drop-leaf table in the kitchen playing with some toys, lost in some imaginary game. A fire was burning in the hearth and, for some strange reason, Dad was at home, and Granddad was with us; both were wearing their 'Sunday best' clothes. For a long time they paced up and down the small room.

Suddenly, a cry came from upstairs and they both rushed towards the sound. Later, someone collected me and I was taken into Mum and Dad's bedroom to meet my new baby brother, Victor James Ayling. I glanced at the small face with dark hair but quickly lost interest

when Mum gave me a rag doll she had sewn herself;
Sally was made out of old black stockings with woollen
hair and features and was wearing a knitted dress. I
loved her, but sadly, as the months went by her skin
turned green.

Peering out of the window I saw two black cars; one
must have been the doctor's and the other, the midwife's. Whenever I thought about my own birth I imagined it had been the same as this.

My brother and I were both named after celebrities of
our time. I was named after Anona Winn, an Australian
singer and actress and, by 1947, a radio personality on
Twenty Questions. When I was young, I hated my name.
All the girls at school had nice, ordinary names like
Susan, Jennifer, Mary and Gillian. I dreaded the first day
of term with a new teacher. We always had to say our
full name out loud.

'Anona Joan Ayling.'

'What?'

'Anona,' I'd repeat, embarrassed.

Victor was named after Victor Sylvester, the band
leader. He was a very sweet baby but I was not very
interested in him as I had my own busy life to get on
with. I had started attending a nursery school two mornings a week. Mum had no friends with children for me
to play with, so presumably felt I was bored and needed
company.

We would walk over a nearby field, past the bomb
crater, to Mrs Powell's cottage in Chalk Pit Lane. She
taught about six children reading and writing and I was
proud of my attempts – even though my first line of
writing would start at the top left-hand corner and finish at the bottom right-hand corner. In fact, I was very
annoyed on my first day at proper school, St Lawrence's
Primary School in Effingham, when all we seemed to do

was play in the sandpit and sit in the Wendy House. I felt much too advanced for that, with all my writing and reading skills!

St Lawrence's was a little country village school and I had many local friends. I did not turn out to be academic but usually received a prize at the end of term for 'Being Willing and Helpful'. My parents also sent me to Sunday school at St Lawrence's Church. I later joined the choir. I must admit I enjoyed going to church more for the social side and as an excuse for being out of the house than for any religious experience.

As my circle widened with school and church, and particularly when I was welcomed into the homes of my friends, I began to see how other families lived; this made me realise that our home life was not the norm. To the outside world we probably appeared fine, but that was because no one was allowed to see in. What nobody knew was that we had a horrible creature living with us and its name was *fear*. Our lives were regulated by many petty rules – some may not seem unreasonable as every child needs boundaries and guidelines. But others were.

In the morning, we would get up, get dressed and go downstairs and not be allowed to return upstairs. (Fortunately, the bathroom was downstairs.) The reason given was, 'You'll wear out the stair carpet.' Also, I was not allowed to listen to the radio. I remember even in my teens, sitting doing my homework at the kitchen table with the radio to my right; I'd see Dad gardening so would tune into Radio Luxembourg, then quickly switch it off if he walked back to the house.

Everything we did had a rule attached to it: eating and washing, talking, sleeping, even reading and going to the toilet. When reading a book, as we did every evening, we were not allowed to turn the corner of the page over or use a bookmark. Dad said we were not really reading properly if we could not remember where we were. In the toilet, only two sheets of Izal paper could be used at a time, and they were horrible shiny sheets, like tracing paper.

It was impossible to remember all the rules and sometimes a new one would appear when you were least expecting it. Then, Dad's wrath would be vented on us, usually verbally. He would shout and call us every name he could think of, every second word a swear word: 'You stupid ********** idiot, can't you do anything properly?'

After being told many times how stupid, useless, ugly and wicked I was, I began to believe it.

Dad was rarely pleasant to Mum or Vic, either. But for some reason he just seemed to *hate* me.

The three of us would be in the kitchen when Dad came home from work. When we heard the sound of his work boots coming around the corner of the house we would seize up, look quickly around the room to see that nothing was out of place that would annoy him, then wait with baited breath to see what kind of a day he'd had and how that would affect us. On one occasion I had been playing on the floor with some very cheap, pink, plastic dolls' house furniture. He trod straight on the toys and crushed them into small pieces.

'Oh, Dad!' I cried.

But my tears meant nothing. He ground the broken toys into the lino.

'You should not have left them in my way!'

I never knew when a beating would happen. Sometimes he would use his hand but often it would be his belt or the strap he used to sharpen his cut-throat razor. I did not understand why I was always in trouble and, as I got older, I would try not to cry in his presence and refused to cower to him. I would stare at him in defiance. This would make him worse and he would put his face a few inches away from me and shout, 'Do not look at me in that tone of voice!'

Sometimes he realised he had gone too far and apologised. This made me despise him even more.

How did this lifestyle affect us? Dad only hit Vic once, but so violently that Vic fell backwards into the fire. He was not badly burnt but Dad obviously panicked, and said, 'I won't do that again, son.' Still, Vic became a very frightened, nervous little boy and clung to Mum for reassurance. Mum was stoic; she tried to make the best of things and keep the peace. But I would take every opportunity to be away from home. As we were not allowed to have friends to the house to play, girl friends would knock on the front door, run back and stand behind the gate when calling for me.

My best friend for a few years was a girl called Susie. I thought she was very romantic and interesting. Susie's parents were gypsies, real ones, with a beautiful old gypsy caravan. She was the youngest of three girls and, when born, was unwell. The family lived further up the hill on land belonging to a kind couple who suggested that Susie slept in their home until she was older. They eventually fostered her and had a lovely bedroom built at the back of their bungalow for her. She saw her mum and dad every day and seemed to enjoy the best of both worlds.

One day, while walking through the woods, Susie and I discussed what it was like for her, being fostered.

Then she said something strange.

'You're adopted, you know.'

I smiled. 'I wish I was.'

I thought about this as I walked home. How wonderful it would be to find I was adopted! I pictured a tall, well-dressed young couple arriving to claim me. They were smiling, with arms outstretched. I knew I would be happy with them. I'd be so thrilled, I wouldn't even wonder why they hadn't kept me . . . But then I came back down to earth with a bump. Everyone said how I took after Dad and I just *knew* I had been born in our house, as Vic had been.

Susie was mad about horses, and before she had her own we would spend hours training her dog to go over very realistic jumps. We had great adventures together and one of my happiest memories is of sitting in her cherry tree picking and eating ripe cherries and spitting out the pips.

Sometimes I took Vic with me when I went out to play. But, being four years younger, he really annoyed me and I didn't always treat him well. Susie's natural parents had a goat, which they housed in an old caravan; so, once, to get some peace, I shut Vic in with it. After hearing a lot of thumping and screaming, I opened the door. Vic stumbled down the steps and the goat got revenge for both of them as it charged towards me and butted me into a barbed wire fence.

I was not actually intentionally naughty – by this time, I was too scared to be – but being a tomboy and having the vast playground of countryside to explore, I often got into mischief.

One beautiful sunny day, I was playing with some older children whose family kept pigs; I sat on the edge of the pigsty and fell backwards. Wearing a summer dress, the mess was mainly on my legs and bottom. The children took me indoors and cleaned me up as much as possible. Then, horrors! I remembered that I was expected for tea at Joan Green's house. Joan's house was identical to ours externally, but inside it couldn't have been more different. Instead of dark brown paint and gaslight, her house was light and pretty. Her mother had a collection of plates arranged on a shelf around the 'dining room', as they called it. Joan's bedroom was also the box room but I noticed she had furniture in it and proper bookshelves and cupboards. I loved visiting the Greens but, that day I sat in silence, embarrassed, eating tiny sandwiches and fairy cakes and smelling of pigs.

In Strathcona Avenue, in a bungalow opposite my grandparents, lived two spinster ladies, the Misses Violet and Ellen Martin. I forget which but one of them taught the piano and for a while I had lessons. Their house was even more Victorian than ours, being stuffed with oversized furniture and so dark that I could hardly read the music. I remember them as kindly ladies but my lessons stopped abruptly when, being a normal child, I one day complained in Dad's hearing of having to practice. I was forbidden to touch our piano ever again and so lost any knowledge I had gained.

Dad had a very stubborn streak; he could hold a grudge for England. If a person upset him, even unintentionally, he would cut them out of his life. During the war, he called in at the William IV pub, which was situated on the side of Box Hill. The landlord was a relation but said he could not serve him as, due to wartime shortages, he only had enough beer for the regulars. Dad hit the roof and that branch of the family was never spoken to again. But alcohol was not a priority with him; the occasional pint with a workmate was all he would have. I think I could have understood his foul temper and violent behaviour if he had been drunk. As it was, he needed no help to be cruel.

Many situations that upset him were dealt with in the same way. From the age of twelve, he had smoked. He would buy tobacco and cigarette paper and roll his own. One day, when he was in his fifties, the price of tobacco went up. He was furious and stopped smoking that day.

Every summer, he would take a week's holiday. We did not go away, but would go out for days. I looked forward to these trips as a break from our usual boring routine. We would leave home early, with me wearing a summer dress and a hand-knitted cardigan. Tucked away in a suitcase would be plastic Macs in case of rain. First we'd catch the bus to Leatherhead, our nearest town, and then the train – steam of course; they did not seem to be in a rush so we always had time to go up to the engine and see the driver, covered with soot. Then off up to London to Madame Tussauds or to an exhibition. To me, a country girl, London seemed huge and also very shabby. From the train we could see the ruined buildings and vast bomb-sites, with some rebuilding going on. The buildings were blackened with the smoke which billowed from the chimneys. For all the shabbiness, London gave me a buzz of excitement; this was where it was all happening.

On other days, we would visit the south coast and even go on a ferry to the Isle of Wight. Because it was such a long trip, we would only have about one hour of sitting on the beach, playing with a bucket and spade, or paddling. Then, it was back on the train to the end of the pier where we would catch the ferry. I always felt sick and often was. Then two trains, a bus and the slow walk up the hill home.

One thing I do remember is that Mum had to get up at the crack of dawn to prepare our food for the day. Banana, cheese and marmite sandwiches, home-made cakes, apples, orange juice for us children, and a thermos of tea for Mum and Dad – this would be placed in the brown suitcase, along with our Macs, and Dad would carry it.

Why did Mum have to go to all this trouble? Well, Dad refused to buy anything that he felt was unnecessary, even a cup of tea. So we had to take it with us!

Years later, I mentioned these outings to Mum.

'They were a nightmare,' she admitted.

A nightmare . . . yes, a good word to use for what was to come next.

4

The Facts of Life

At school, we began to hear rumours of a terrifying event soon to be upon us, the dreaded eleven-plus examination. If you passed, you were assured of a bright future, grammar school and college; perhaps even university and a career in teaching, business or law. If you failed, all you had to look forward to was the local secondary modern with hairdressing and shop work for the girls, and manual, blue-collar work for the boys. Of course, that was not how it always worked out, because many young people blossom later in life, and others cannot cope with the academic world. But for us, the pressure was on.

My friends were happily reporting how their dads had promised them a bike or a watch if they passed. I did not tell them that my dad had promised me a beating if I failed.

Homework was a nightmare. Dad would stand behind me shouting and hitting me when I made mistakes, which I often did, particularly in arithmetic. I could not grasp it at all.

On the day of the exam, I sat staring at the papers, my mind a blank. I must have answered some questions correctly as I only just failed. There were places left at the local grammar school, so some of us took the exam again, with different questions, of course. There was only one thing worse than failing your eleven-plus once and that was failing it twice . . . still, one good thing came of this. Dad had been proved right – apparently I was an idiot, as he had thought. So, he no longer took any interest in my education and did not pressurise Vic into doing more than he could.

The local secondary modern, the Howard of Effingham, was only a few hundred yards down the road from my primary school. It was a scary place, with nearly three hundred pupils – they all seemed like giants. The teachers were stricter and we new children were always getting lost, as we had to move to different classrooms and not stay comfortably in one room with one teacher. At that time, the Howard of Effingham was considered a rough school and corporal punishment was used a lot. (Who would guess that years later it would be one of the top schools in Surrey?) Sadly, my years there were not happy – not because of the school, but because of life at home. I was very depressed and had no incentive to do well. Just getting through each day was enough.

As I had only just failed the eleven-plus, I was put in the 'A' stream. In the first year end-of-term exam, I was third in the class of thirty-five. But by the time I left, I was thirty-second. Because I was tall, it was thought I would be good at sport – I wasn't. However, one year, I found myself competing in the Surrey Sports Day, held at Ronson's Sports Ground in Leatherhead. The girls I was running against from other schools looked at least a year older than me. I was saved from the indignity of coming last when one girl stopped to do up her shoelace.

Some of my friends had record players and had started collecting records. I enjoyed going to their homes and hearing the latest pop stars. Because I was forbidden to listen to the radio, I would creep down the stairs when Mum and Dad had it on and, from the bottom step, I would listen to Cliff Richard singing 'Living Doll'. I quite liked him but my favourite was Elvis.

As we got older, our looks and boys began to be of great importance. I had been told that I was ugly so many times that I believed it. Being one of the tallest in the class, I towered above most of the boys so was always the last to be chosen for country dancing. The National Health metal-framed spectacles I wore did not help, either; I had very bad eyesight and had worn glasses from the age of five. My clothes were old-fashioned and always too big 'so you can grow into them'. We did have a school uniform but not many wore it regularly; I remember nearly dying of embarrassment when singing in a school choir at Epsom Baths – I was the only girl with a blue cardigan amongst a sea of green.

I was very envious of a girl in my class called Christine Dodd. She was very pretty, shorter than me and wore up-to-date clothes, passed down to her from her older sister. She was very popular with the boys; just the kind of girl you could hate if she had not been so nice. We went to Art School together on a Saturday morning (and later, by strange coincidence, she worked for 'my husband-to-be'). Interestingly, when we were both married with children, we met again, and talked about school. I told her how jealous I had been.

She was astounded. 'I always thought you were attractive,' she said. 'When *Wonder Woman*, Linda Carter, came on the television, I was reminded of you.'

Also, years later, I met two other old friends from schooldays, Linda and Shannon. Linda said, 'You always reminded me of a frightened animal.' This was an interesting remark too. Because, the truth was, the bold child had changed into a scared and bemused young girl. Nobody knew what had started to happen to me at home in my early teens; I didn't understand it myself and certainly never talked about it.

I was thirteen years old when, early one Saturday morning, my dad came into my bedroom and shut the door. He knelt down beside the bed and started to kiss me on the lips, while groping at my non-existent breasts. I was not sure what he was doing with his other hand, but his breathing got heavier and he was saying, 'I love you,' which he never *ever* said. Eventually it was over, he went downstairs, and I got up and followed, not knowing what to expect. He was quite calm and pleasant to me that day.

These visits would occur every few weekends over the next two years.

I dreaded those mornings and grew to really hate my father. The only way I could cope was to lie absolutely still with my eyes tight shut and try to block out what was happening. I would frantically search in my mind for something nice or different to think about, somewhere else where I could be. This was not always successful, so later I would mentally put all the horrible things in the black corrugated shed in the garden. This was Dad's domain. I now know that many children who are sexually abused feel that they are to blame but, strangely, I never felt that. It was just another thing that Dad did to me to make me feel worthless and to take away what little self-esteem I had left. It did not occur to me to speak to Mum about what was going on. Because of our rules, I knew she'd be downstairs getting breakfast ready when my dad was upstairs with me. I also somehow knew that she would not want to know about it.

Truthfully, I did not know what to think. I had no understanding of what was happening but I knew it was wrong and I hated it. Sex education was in short supply in the late fifties; one day, I even asked, 'Mum, Dad, what are the facts of life?' and Dad snapped, 'If you don't know now, you never will.' I also made the mistake of asking Mum – in front of him – if I could have a bra. He muttered, 'What are you going to put in it, potatoes?'

I was a very late developer and did not even know about periods. One day, walking home from school I saw blood on my legs. I thought I was dying and ran home, sobbing.

Mum was very embarrassed. 'This will happen every month now,' she said, handing me some horrible sanitary towels and a thick belt to hang them on.

The girls at school would talk about babies and where they came from. But we weren't sure about it, thinking no woman in her right mind would have more than one baby after such a terrible thing happened to her. We certainly had no idea of how babies were conceived. Then, there was a scandal; an older girl suddenly left school. Apparently a dead baby had been found in her wardrobe. Her mother had smelt it.

At this point in my life, I had a paper round on weekdays so earned a little money to spend on myself. The fashion for white broderie anglaise blouses and full, gathered skirts worn with a wide belt was all the rage. The skirt had to stick out so a net petticoat was needed. Once you washed it all the stiffness went so you had to buy another and then continually starch them to keep the desired body. I loved fashion and would spend hours drawing clothes and shoes, imagining myself wearing my creations. It was a great way to escape from what was happening at home.

Reading was another way of escape. I devoured books, spending all my spare money on them, and devising my own library system with the small collection of books on my shelf. I would even creep into the front room to read Dad's collection of *The Great War* volumes – with all the gory pictures of the dreaded Hun.

But I was desperately unhappy at home. Apart from what was happening with my father – I felt Mum should have been protecting me – I felt my mother never treated me like a daughter. We did not go shopping together or talk about life, boys or any girly things. She had no interest in clothes or make-up and gave me no help or advice as I grew into a young woman. I resented both my parents and plotted how I could run away. The problem was that I had no knowledge of towns or cities so the only place I could run away to was the country – and I knew how hard it would be to survive with no shelter in the cold and wet.

One day, while walking back to our house through the woods, I felt so desperate to escape that I even considered killing myself. After seriously thinking over the various ways of doing this – slitting my wrists, hanging myself, swallowing lots of tablets – I realised they were all painful and I was too much of a coward.

During this time, I had nightmares nearly every night. One was of our house on fire; I was trapped in my bedroom with no way of escape. In the other, I was being chased along a narrow track with banks and could only go forwards. My pursuer was a man dressed in black, riding a black motorbike. I could hear the sound of the bike getting nearer but my legs just would not go any faster. I eventually discovered how to deal with these nightmares. I would, while the dream was happening, say to myself, 'It's only a dream,' shut my eyes, clench my fists and jump up and down until I woke myself up.

I also lost any interest I'd had in God. One night, whilst walking home after the evening service, I suddenly realised that for all the hours I had spent in church, I had never experienced God. Surely church was the place it would have happened? I had even been confirmed in the Anglican Church but felt no different. Was Christianity all about singing hymns and listening to boring sermons? It appeared so. Consequently, with all the knowledge and insight of a thirteen-year-old, I decided I was an atheist. Then, looking up at the sky, I panicked; the stars were bright and the moon was shining. If there was no God the whole universe could spin out of control and destroy us all. I felt it was lonely and scary being an atheist.

'If I can only get through the next few years,' I thought, 'I can be independent one day.'

Dad was forever telling me, 'When we die, Victor will get the house. You'll have a husband to look after you.' So perhaps there was hope after all – maybe I would get married and have a family. I vowed it would be nothing like the one I'd grown up in. My children would not fear me *or* their father. We would have fun together and their friends would always be welcome.

Around this time I started to have a daydream. I would have a house and gather in it children of all ages. They would arrive in a terrible state but I would bathe them and dress them in beautiful warm clothes, and feed them with healthy but tasty food. They would have lovely bedrooms with many toys. I would teach them and care for them and they would be safe and happy. I would replay that daydream, naming the children and seeing them grow up.

When I was fourteen, my childhood, such as it was, came to an abrupt end. Dad suddenly accosted me in the kitchen.

'You can leave school on your fifteenth birthday,' he told me. 'I'm not going to support you any longer.'

This was quite a shock. We were all studying for the RSA exams to be taken in the next year, and my birthday was fast approaching. I would have to leave before Christmas.

On the one hand, it was good to be told I could leave school but on the other, the sense of rejection was great. It was yet another way for my dad to let me know I was of no value and was on my own.

The thought of going out into the big wide world was frightening.

5

An Appointment with Destiny

Someone must have notified the school that I was leaving, as I was quite quickly booked into a meeting with the careers officer.

'What would you like to do for a job?' he asked.

'I don't know,' I replied. 'I haven't thought about it.'

'What are your best subjects?'

I thought hard. 'Umm, English and Art.'

Art was my favourite. I was not that good at drawing or painting but had an eye for colour and design.

'How about being a window dresser?' suggested the careers officer.

'Yes, fine!' I agreed at once. I knew I had to get a job fast.

An appointment was made with the general manager at H.L. Reid and Co., a department store in Epsom. I was very nervous but got the job – not as a window dresser (no vacancies, apparently), but as a junior on the fashion floor. My wage per week would be £3. 10s. I bought a white blouse and a black cardigan from the drapers in Leatherhead and, using a Simplicity pattern, managed to sew a straight black skirt for my uniform. And on 31 December 1962, aged just fifteen, I started work.

Under the strict eye of Mrs Neadam, the manageress, I began to learn many new skills – how to use a phone, how to vacuum the carpets, how to tie parcels. The clothes did not interest me at all; they were designed for much older ladies and were very expensive. Besides, as a junior, I did not even speak to the customers. A very strict hierarchy was upheld. It was a bit like *Are You Being Served?*, but with fewer laughs.

There is a verse in the Bible that says, 'What was meant for evil, God has turned for good'.[1] Dad did not have my best interests at heart when he made me finish my schooling and work to support myself. But, in fact, that very first day turned out to be the most important in my life. *Someone* was on my case. I had an appointment with destiny.

On that first day, I was sent up to the canteen for a coffee break. Feeling very shy, I stood in the queue.

The young man in front of me turned and smiled.

'Hi, is this your first day?'

'Yes.'

'My name's Jerry. Come and sit with us.'

A table full of young people welcomed me, and cigarettes were soon being passed around. I took one, puffed . . . and choked. It became obvious that everyone except Jerry smoked and you were expected to pass them round. I quickly did my sums; the weekly bus fares came to over £1 and all my food, toiletries and clothes would have to come out of the rest. I would have to be a non-smoker.

Jerry was a very friendly and outgoing type of person. He had a way of making you feel as if you were the most important person in the room. He was a window-dresser in the display department, very popular with all the staff for working hard, and always brightening up the day with his jokes. He was also respected for his strong faith. He was a committed Christian and not ashamed of it.

I, of course, as an atheist, had no interest in religion. But I was quite impressed when, on the first day, Jerry told me of a motorbike accident he'd had the year before. His parents were told that he had only three hours to live but he had survived and had been named 'the miracle boy' at Atkinson Morley's Hospital in Wimbledon.

I liked Jerry very much but soon developed a crush on his boss, a tall, dark, rather dashing man in his midtwenties. But the boss wasn't interested in me. So, being the only girl there without a boyfriend, I invented one. I called him Colin and would mention occasionally that I would be seeing him that night. It soon got too complicated so I announced I had finished with him.

My friends from school and I still met up. Sometimes we went to a dance held at the Barn Hall in nearby Fetcham. Usually the boys would stand in a huddle eyeing up the girls while we would dance around a pile of handbags. Every now and again, a boy would ask me out to the cinema at Leatherhead, saying, 'I'll meet you inside.' Then I would catch the bus from Effingham, paying a child's fare, put on my make-up, and go in to see an adult film. I did have trouble seeing them, though, because I refused to wear my glasses. I was very aware of the popular saying, 'Boys never make passes at girls who wear glasses'. Perhaps I should have kept them on. I hated it when a boy put his arm around me and even tried to kiss me.

The winter of 1962 to 1963 was a hard one, thick snow and bitterly cold. Often my bus could not make the last part of the journey to work in Epsom, and we would all get off and walk the last couple of miles. Work was quite tiring as I seemed to do all the running around; also, as a shop assistant, I was never allowed to sit down. We only had Wednesday afternoon and Sunday off, and we would also work late on a Thursday evening.

I made many friends among the younger staff and the older ladies were very kind to me. I soon learned that swearing and calling everyone 'mate' was not acceptable in polite society and, by watching how people behaved, I slowly began to mature.

Home was still not a happy place but the lodgings available in Epsom cost more than I earned, so leaving was not an option. Dad would still get into terrible tempers and, for the first time, people outside of my home discovered what was happening, for sometimes I had to go to work with bruises on my face.

As the months went by, I began to feel very attracted to Jerry. He had an amazing personality and that 'something special' that drew me to him. I, of course, dropped a hint to one of the display team, and she came back with, 'Jerry'd like to ask you out, but he's a Christian, you know.'

'I don't care if he's a Buddhist!' I replied.

Our first date was very romantic. We saw the show *The Sound of Music* at the Palace Theatre in London. On the train coming back, Jerry held my hand and later kissed me goodnight.

A few days later, he took me home to meet his parents, Mr and Mrs Coates. They were lovely and made me very welcome. He had a brother, Roy, who was the same age as me and still at school, and a sister, Miriam, one year older. Miriam was very sophisticated; she knew how to put on make-up, do her hair and dress well and also had a boyfriend with a motorbike . . . the one Jerry had crashed.

I began to meet Jerry's friends from his church, the Christian Brethren in Cobham, near where the Coates family lived in Stoke D'Abernon. Jerry's best friend, Brian, lived next door and attended the same church. With Brian's girlfriend, Jenny, we soon became a foursome.

Then, the church erected a marquee on Cobham Recreation Ground and held a series of evangelistic meetings. The speaker was a Mr Jim Smyth. Our next few dates were tea at Mr and Mrs Coates's, then a walk into Cobham for the meeting. After a few hymns (different to the ones we sang at St Lawrence's Church) and some prayers, Mr Smyth would preach. Although you could say there was quite a lot of 'hell fire and damnation', something in his talks touched me. For the first time I heard the gospel and understood what it really meant – how human beings had been created in God's image but sin had come in and spoilt our relationship with him, how God the Father had sent his Son Jesus to live and die for us, and how we could tell God we were sorry and ask for Jesus to be central in our lives to help us to be his true disciples.

At the end of each meeting, there was an opportunity to pray with Mr Smyth. One evening, I spoke with Jerry and Mr Smyth and, with their help, committed my life to God.

I did not feel any different to start with. I believed in my head that things had changed but about three weeks later it seemed that my new belief dropped from my brain to my heart. I began to sense God's love and had a peace that I had not known before.

I was told it was very important to share my new faith with others and, of course, the first people I did this with were my family.

Dad went absolutely mad.

'Who are you that God would be interested in you?'

Perhaps I was stupid but I would read my Bible in front of him and openly talk about what I believed and how God had answered my prayers. This would make him even more violent and aggressive; it was as if something within him was reacting to even the mention of God and Jesus.

I had no idea how a new Christian should behave. A few months earlier, a friend from school and I had booked a week's holiday at Butlin's Holiday Camp in Bognor Regis. The time had now arrived; neither of us had been away from home on our own before and did not know what to expect. I had read in a magazine that a holiday romance could ruin a girl's relationship with her boyfriend back home so was determined not to have one. We had not realised that the whole point of teenagers going to Butlin's was for boys to pick up girls – and if romance wasn't on the agenda, sex certainly was. After a series of very scary dates, there was no way we were going to meet any of the boys we went out with again! So I was very pleased and proud to write a postcard to Jerry saying

Having a lovely time. Weather not too bad. Don't worry, I've been out with a different boy every night.

He must have wondered what he'd got himself into.

Gerald, as I now called him (he was only Jerry at work), was promoted to display manager aged only nineteen. I left H.L. Reid's and started work at 'Claudia', a dress shop in Epsom. I was still a junior but I could dress the windows and earn a little more money. I also went back to Art School part-time, to display classes.

It was during this time that I was nearly killed three times in one week. Coming out of Claudia one lunchtime, I looked right, left and right again, then stepped into the road – just as a car appeared as if from nowhere. It missed me by inches. I was shocked and other people on the kerb asked where the car had come from.

A couple of days later, I was the only person in the showroom, just sitting at the desk doing some paperwork, when I felt the urge to get up and walk to the back of the shop, towards the fitting rooms. As I walked away, I heard a terrific roar. Looking back, I saw the ceiling collapse. Big chunks fell just where I'd been sitting.

The last event took place at home one evening. Mum, Dad and Vic were out and I was drying my hair in the kitchen. Again for no reason I felt I must walk out of the room to the scullery. I opened the door and saw flames pouring from the old-fashioned paraffin heater Mum had left on to heat the room. Quite stupidly, I picked up the heater by its handle, flames licking around my hand, and threw it out of the back door. Fortunately, at the time that part of the garden was just dirt so no lasting damage was done.

I was a nervous wreck by the end of that week!

The Brethren Church, or Assembly as it was known, was a very close-knit community – about forty members, mainly middle-aged and older people. Gerald was an excellent speaker and communicator. Soon we began to gather together local young people and, with children and teenagers from the church families, formed a youth group. Preaching the gospel was our main priority.

The church Bible studies were good. I began to think that after a few years I would know everything there was to know. One thing bothered me, though. I had been reading in 1 Corinthians chapter 12 about the gifts of the Spirit. This was amazing; God, through his Holy Spirit, could give us the gift to speak in tongues, prophesy and even to pray for healing. Standing at a bus stop one evening I asked Gerald when we would start to see these things at our church.

He answered, sadly, that he had thought the same but the church elders had been annoyed when he asked about it.

'You young people,' they'd said, 'you always want more. These gifts were for the Early Church.'

Although my faith in God was growing stronger, I still had many emotional needs. I found it hard to trust people for fear they would reject me. Showing affection and just 'being myself' was hard. However, I read in the New Testament how Jesus broke through the cultural barriers of his time, and related to women and children as equal with men. This gave me hope. But unfortunately, I had joined a church where women were *not* considered equal. Unless it was a ladies' meeting, only men were allowed to take part in our services, praying or preaching. Women had to wear hats or scarves and keep quiet. Certainly no form of leadership was considered for them. So, I was thought of as second-class at home, and now I was second-class at church, the one place I could have been liberated.

To be considered 'worldly' was a great sin. That cut out all the fun things like dancing, going to the cinema, wearing make-up and, especially, drinking alcohol and smoking cigarettes. Also, 'Keeping the Sabbath holy' was essential. Other than going to church meetings and eating, everything else was banned. No watching television on Sunday, listening to the radio, mowing the lawn – and certainly no shopping.

Gerald and I did not really mind these restrictions. We wanted to serve God and do his will. If that was it, it was fine by us. The only problem was, we would judge other Christians who did not live by our standards.

Yet again, my life was governed by rules. Not biblical rules, but ones made up by human beings, although we did not realise that at the time.

Endnote

[1] See Genesis 50:20.

6

Married Life

Mr and Mrs Coates, as I always called them, were very good to me. After work on a Saturday, Gerald and I would go to their house. I would stay Saturday night and not return home until Sunday night.

Transport was always a big problem. Although our homes were not far away from one another, the journey back to my parents' house was very complicated. Soon after 9 p.m., Gerald and I would catch the train from Stoke D'Abernon to Effingham Junction, then the train to Leatherhead. He would make the journey back while I walked to the bus station to catch the bus to the part of Effingham I lived in.

One evening, the bus was very late and I arrived home after the curfew Dad had set for me. I was never given my own key and the back door was locked. I sat on the step, crying, not knowing what to do. After about half an hour, Mum came down and let me in. She had been waiting for Dad to fall asleep.

On another occasion, Gerald was unwell and I made the journey on my own. It was a nightmare. While at Effingham Junction, alone in the waiting room, a middle-aged man came in and started to talk to me. I did not mind that, but then he began to get too friendly. I was relieved when the train drew in. He was obviously not getting on my train so I relaxed in a compartment on my own. I could not believe it when a man joined me at Bookham station, sat next to me, and started touching me. I was franticly trying to escape when the train arrived at Leatherhead, and other people getting on board gave me the chance to jump off. Unbelievably, walking down the hill to the bus station, I was accosted by a man who appeared out of the bushes. I had had enough by then.

'Get lost, you pervert!' I yelled.

He ran away.

By the time I arrived home I was as white as a sheet and shaking. Although nervous about their reaction, I had to tell Mum and Dad what had happened. I was shocked when Dad was very sympathetic and angry that I had been through all that – after all he had done to me! Still, it was not until much later that I realised I had been in more danger at home than on the streets.

My diary entry on Friday 14 August 1964 reads

Went to funfair at Dreamland in Margate, Gerald asked me to marry him.

I was sixteen. We had gone on holiday with Brian and Jenny, staying at a bed and breakfast in Broadstairs, girls in one room, boys in another. The romantic moment actually occurred in one of the windbreak shelters.

'If we were able to,' said Gerald, 'would you marry me?'

'Yes,' I replied, simply.

We were engaged a year later. Gerald visited my parents – a very rare event, as he was never made welcome and my father hated him. We stood in the kitchen and Gerald asked for Dad's permission to marry me.

Dad's reply was one of his many sayings.
'Well, you've made your bed, now you must lie on it.'
We hadn't, actually.

I had started work at Harvey's Department Store in
Guildford, now the House of Fraser, first in the linen
department, then in the display department. Travelling
to work on the bus on my first day I was introduced to a
girl named Mary Limmer (later to become Mary Hood).
She was a window dresser at Harvey's and had been a
pupil at the Howard of Effingham. I later trained under
Mary in display. It was one of the most creative jobs I
had; the department was quite large, we had sixty windows to dress – the store had a beautiful arcade at that
time. There was even a studio which made all the props
for our displays. We had quite a free rein to be creative.

I was amazed to find that Mary seemed to be a very
committed Christian. She went to an Anglican church,
drank wine, danced and went to the cinema! I could not
understand this worldliness but recognised that she
loved God as I did. We became close friends and, one
Sunday, Mary came to our Brethren service.

The elder preaching that night was, as usual, talking
about all the things we should not be doing.

Suddenly, he announced loudly, 'No one ever became
a Christian in a cinema!'

Mary, who didn't know that women were not allowed
to speak, called out, 'I did!'

It transpired that she had gone to watch the film *The
Greatest Story Ever Told* and was so affected by the life of
Jesus that she committed herself to him.

Mary and I would have great times sharing our faith
with the team we worked with, and quite a few became
Christians. Mary later joined a little group meeting in
our home, and is still one of my closest friends.

Because Gerald and I both worked in department stores we were able to get a discount on items we needed for our future home. During our two-year engagement, we gradually bought china, bedding and even furniture. As Gerald was a manager, he was able to get an even larger reduction. And I was very pleased when I found a white silk wedding dress with matching pink bridesmaid's dress in the sale at Harvey's at £5 each.

The wedding itself would be a simple affair to be taken by Mr Evan Evans at Cannon Court Evangelical Church in Fetcham, as at the time we were no longer in the official Brethren Assembly.

Our pre-marriage talk with Mr and Mrs Evans was interesting as Mr Evans read from the Bible about Mary, Martha and Lazarus opening their home to Jesus and the disciples. I do not think he realised that he was being prophetic but he encouraged us to do the same, something we took seriously.

Dad said he would not have anything to do with the wedding and would not attend. But the week before, he changed his mind and I had to quickly let down the turn-ups and move the buttons on the suit he wore to his own wedding, thirty years earlier.

Finding a home to rent was proving difficult. We strongly felt we should live in Cobham. At that time, next to Knightsbridge, it was known as the most expensive area to live in. One day, Dad asked me where we were going to live and I told him it seemed that God wanted us to live in Cobham.

'Why would God be interested in you? You'll never have anywhere to live. You wait. On your wedding day I'll remind you of this conversation.'

Just before our wedding day, we found a thirties' terraced house – 41 Tartar Road, in Cobham. It belonged to a property company and was available to rent. We could just about afford the amount, it was £4 a week, and we had the basics to furnish it.

I can't say I enjoyed our wedding day. I was still painfully shy and hated having to be the centre of attention. But all went well. The chef at Harvey's made the cake and the photographer was a friend of Mary's. Miriam was my bridesmaid and Roy, Gerald's best man.

Dad gave me away – something he had been looking forward to, I'm sure, but probably not for the same reasons a 'normal' father would look forward to such a day.

Our honeymoon was spent on a boat on the River Thames. Although it was March (just in time to get a tax rebate), the weather was glorious. We chugged up to Goring and then back to Thames Ditton.

Gerald's dad collected us from the boatyard looking rather worried. Of course, my dad had not been able to remind me of his words on my wedding day as we had our own little home to move into. But Mr Coates had opened a letter for Gerald by mistake and found it was from the property company – because of government policy changes on housing, they had decided not to let the house but to sell it.

We were disappointed but not downhearted. After staying at a bed and breakfast in Guildford for three weeks, we moved in with the Coates family. They were all great about it but it was not an ideal situation; poor Roy had to sleep in the front room, while I shared with Gerald. We continued to look for a place in Cobham, but eventually gave in and went to look at a small flat in Leatherhead. It was unsuitable in every way, double the price, very small and fully furnished but we felt we had to move somewhere.

Gerald was at work in his display studio in Epsom, ready to leave for an appointment in Leatherhead to sign a six-month lease. As he locked the door behind him, the phone rang. He hesitated; he might be late for the 6.30 appointment.

'No,' he decided, 'better answer it.'

He went back into the room and picked up the phone.

'Mr Coates, are you still interested in 41 Tartar Road?'

'Yes!'

'Come and collect the keys on Monday. It's yours.'

This was the story of our life; quite miraculously, God always provided just what we needed at the time.

Our first few years of married life were not easy. I was still very battered after my years of living with my parents. I found it very hard to accept that I was attractive to Gerald and of any value to anyone else. The slightest criticism would send me into a spiral of rejection and negativity.

It took me a long time to enjoy making love. Although I loved Gerald, I felt it was something forced upon me and I would often have flashbacks to the times my dad would take advantage of me. I had told Gerald about the abuse but never in detail so he did not understand why I did not want to be kissed on the lips.

I was also very scared of the possibility of violence. Gerald only had to playfully pat me on the bottom for me to react badly. Later, when we owned a television set, I could never watch a programme featuring child abuse. If I happened to be caught out by something suddenly coming on the screen, I would say, 'That's all wrong. She would never turn her back on him like that. You have to keep your eye on someone you fear *all* the time. You never know when they'll strike.'

Like most young married couples, we were very short of money. The house had no heating. We would light a fire in the front room and move a two-bar electric fire to any other room in use. With no refrigerator, I bought our food daily and in the winter would leave the milk outside. On Mondays, my day off work, I would wash the laundry by hand. That was fine for small items but sheets and towels were hard work. With vinyl floor covering, we had no need for a vacuum cleaner and, for any phone calls we needed to make, there was the phone box in the next road.

Although our home was very basic it was ours to use, as Mr Evans had suggested in his pre-marriage talk, to be hospitable and to welcome others. So, right from the beginning of our life in our new home, we had people staying with us. Roger Ingold was the first. He had become a Christian at a coffee bar we had arranged for young people in Cobham. After growing up in a children's home, he had to leave at sixteen and he was lodging at a bed and breakfast. Feeling Roger needed a more normal family home, we invited him to stay. I am pleased to say we are still good friends today.

With the best of intentions, we perhaps naively invited homeless people to live with us. Believing that friends, a roof over their head and a proper job would help these young men, we were disappointed when after a few weeks they would walk out taking most of our meagre possessions with them. One young man would regularly disappear up to London for a day or two; we later discovered he was a male prostitute. Another arrived wearing clothes so filthy I spent about thirty minutes trying to wash them in the sink; the water ran black. We made a big mistake with him – we found him a job in a local off-licence, not realising he was an alcoholic.

After eighteen months of marriage, our first baby arrived. Paul was born on Gerald's twenty-fourth birthday, and I came out of hospital on my twenty-first. We did not worry about being young, having no experience of babies and having no money. We were married; it seemed the most natural thing in the world to have a baby.

I was very sick for several months, as I was with all of our children. I had finished working at Harvey's in Guildford and was now working as a receptionist and shampooer at a hairdresser's in Cobham. The smell of the perm lotion was so strong I would be shampooing a client's hair when the nausea began.

'Excuse me one moment, madam,' I'd say, as I rushed to the back of the salon to be sick.

One day, feeling wretched, I'd walked down to the high street to buy some food. Attracted by a bunch of the first daffodils of the season, I'd bought them instead of the food. The pleasure I had from those daffodils was out of all proportion, but I discovered that day that it was as important to feed the soul as the stomach.

It was a great blessing that Paul was such a good and compliant child. A first baby is so special; I remember looking at him asleep and feeling such a love that my chest ached.

A month after Paul was born we spent Christmas Day with Gerald's parents. Mr Coates was going to drive us to visit my family on Boxing Day. That morning we woke up to a beautiful Christmas scene, with thick snow; it was impossible to get the car out of the drive. Fortunately we were able to ring Mum and Dad's neighbours to let them know we would not be able to make the journey. We were never invited to visit at Christmas again.

Gerald's parents both died when Paul was quite young, and my parents showed no interest in him, but he was surrounded by uncles and aunts in the form of all the young people in our home. We thought it would be nice to have another child to keep him company and, two years and four days later, Simon was born. We had a Christian speaker from Bath staying with us at the time and, when I went into labour in the middle of the night, Steve drove me to the hospital.

When we arrived there the nurse said, 'Your husband can come in, too.'

'Oh no,' I replied. 'He's not my husband.'

She was shocked. Well – this was a while ago!

Poor little Simon, apparently the placenta had not been working properly for the last two weeks and he had been slowly starving. His little legs were thin, his stomach distended and his head had begun to shrink. I was feeding him one day in hospital when I noticed he had webbing between two fingers and two toes. A paediatrician was sent for and we were advised to have his hand operated on when he was four. On returning home, he caught a bad cold and developed a hernia.

Mum had looked after Paul while I was in hospital giving birth to Simon. That occasion and once, many years later, when she had our third child, Jonathan, for a weekend, were the only times she babysat for them. I did ask her one other time but she said, 'No,' – I think it made life with Dad much too difficult. I did feel very hurt that they did not want to spend time with the boys, but really, it was only to be expected.

We had been married for several years before we could afford for Gerald to take driving lessons. The day after he passed, we were offered an elderly Hillman Minx from some friends in Canterbury. When it broke down – as it frequently did – we would get out of the car, lay hands on the bonnet, pray, and it would start again.

Then, one day, Gerald was returning home with some visiting pastors from Argentina when one of the passengers heard pieces from under the car falling onto the road. The vehicle ground to a halt and Gerald collected the parts and put them into a brown paper bag. The men gathered around and prayed for the car to start. It did and they drove to our house. I saw it pull up outside and the men fall out laughing. But that was the end of that car; it never moved again!

7

Living by Faith

We had learnt many good things from the Brethren but, for several reasons, we'd left the church. Our horizons had broadened and we now mixed with Christians from other denominations, realising that we did *not* have the monopoly on the truth.

We were, however, disillusioned with the established church with all its pomp and ceremony so looked into the Bible to learn how the early Christians lived and worshipped. We read how they had met in one another's homes, preached in the open air, shared all they had and saw miracles happen. We felt we should live by their example. So with our three friends, Roger and two sisters, Penny and Linda, we met on a Sunday morning in our front room to study the Bible, pray and worship God. We were very evangelistic in sharing our faith, so soon others became Christians and joined us.

As the number of young people we were responsible for grew, Gerald realised he would have to leave his full-time job. He started work as a postman in the Cobham area. At that time, they did a lot of overtime so it was an early start in all weathers. Arriving home at 2 p.m., he would usually fall asleep over his lunch and then study for the rest of the afternoon. He was getting quite well

known as a public speaker so some evenings and weekends he would be away. After about eighteen months he
no longer had time to even work as a postman.

Because we did not belong to a traditional church,
there was no financial support. But we had read a book
by an amazing Chinese Christian called Watchman Nee,
who lived through persecution in China and told how
he would not tell people of his needs but would pray
and leave it to God. This way of life was called 'living by
faith'. Gerald would occasionally be given some money
after speaking, but it was often 'Take whatever is in the
collection' – 2s. 6d. and a couple of buttons!

To supplement our income, I would do dressmaking
and alterations after the boys went to bed and Gerald
worked nights at a local petrol station. The manager was
the father of Penny and Linda, two of the original five
who'd first met in our home. He was not happy about
the girls being involved with us as he thought that we
were some strange sect. But he did say, 'I don't like that
Gerald Coates but I must admit the nights he works are
the only ones when the sales of petrol and the money in
the till match up.'

It was exciting but nerve-racking, praying in enough
money to live, but it certainly taught us a wonderful les-
son: if we could trust God for the next meal, we could
trust him for anything.

We always paid our bills, but usually it was at the last
moment. One winter's day, the doorbell rang. It was a
man from the electricity board to turn off the electricity;
he was nearly in tears as he looked at me holding Simon,
with Paul beside me.

'I hate this job, especially with young 'uns in the
house.'

'Don't worry,' I said, 'we've paid it.'

Fortunately we had the receipt to prove it.

We never went without a meal but sometimes they were very unusual. One day, however, there was only a bag of sugar and some rice in the larder. The milkman was due to call for his money and I was in tears.

'I don't mind for myself,' I said to Gerald, 'but I don't want the boys to go without.'

The bell rang and I went to answer the door. I was ready to say, 'I'm sorry. I haven't got the money this week,' but I found the milkman putting a cardboard box full of groceries on the step!

'A lady down the road paid your bill,' he said.

Travelling to speak at church meetings was a big problem with no money. One time, Gerald had been invited to spend a few days preaching at a church near Northampton. We gathered all the money we had, and he gave me some for food; all that was left was enough for the bus fare to Cobham Railway Station. He would have to trust God for the rest of the journey. As Gerald stepped onto the bus in Cobham high street, Roger, who no longer lived with us, ran out of the electrical shop he worked in.

'I think God's told me to give you this,' he gasped, and stuffed some notes into Gerald's hand.

Not all our answers to prayer were as painless. Back when Gerald was working in the post office, sorting the mail, an insurance salesman came in. Insurance was not something we thought about but the salesman was very convincing.

'Only £1 to pay today and, if you have an accident and are off work, you can be compensated,' he said.

Just to get rid of him, Gerald put down the money and signed the form.

The very next day he was on his round, cycling down the Byfleet Road in Cobham, when he was hit by a car and taken to hospital with a broken leg and many cuts and bruises. The insurance company covered all our bills as he was off work for several weeks.

Cycling could be a blessing, though. Another day, he'd been making his deliveries along an exclusive road in Cobham, when he found himself singing in a strange language. He had been what the Bible calls 'baptised in the Spirit' and was speaking in tongues. We had read in the Acts of the Apostles[1] that the Early Church had experienced this as they gathered on the day of Pentecost. God blessed all our fellowship with this gift, and we became what is now called 'charismatic'.

Every evening, our house was full of youngsters; cars and motorbikes roared away in the early hours, much to the horror of our neighbours. We could not afford to offer much in the way of refreshments, just tea or coffee with broken biscuits – yes, you could buy them already broken, so much cheaper. Ours was the only home that could be used and was not very large, so when the numbers rose to thirty, we had to hire a hall to meet in. This of course meant we incurred expenses and had to get ourselves organised and open a bank account. But to do that, we needed a name. We came up with the 'Cobham Christian Fellowship'. This had not been in our thoughts at all. Without planning to, we had become a house church!

Our little church grew from faith and friendship – living with one another, going on holiday, helping one another financially . . . I'm afraid, in our youthful ignorance we alienated many of the local people who were not part of the 'Cobham Christian Fellowship'. Some very weird rumours spread around the town. One was that Cliff Richard had bought all our houses. 'If only!' we laughed. But another was very upsetting. The local vicar and his wife had become good friends, but tragically, the vicar had become very depressed and took his own life. We were devastated; not only had we lost a wonderful man but rumour had it that he had wanted to leave his church and join us but we had refused him – completely untrue.

As time went on, a basic income was arranged for us, which Gerald could top up with his ministry further afield. Other men and women were appointed to share in the responsibility of leading the growing church.

We had discovered that we were not the only group meeting in homes and halls in an informal way. Connections were being made with other house church leaders and we met many incredible people who we continue to share our lives with now, including John and Christine Noble and their family. John was only a few years older than Gerald but soon became a father figure and advisor to him.

Worship and music was a very important part of church life and we were blessed by many of the modern-day hymn writers and musicians. A large group of young people moved to Cobham from Plymouth to be with us. One young couple were Noel and Tricia Richards. Gerald and Noel made a great team, Gerald preaching and Noel leading the worship as they travelled at home and abroad. Noel and Tricia became two of our closest friends and Gerald joined them in writing several worship songs and hymns.

Because of Gerald's work, we have had the opportunity of meeting many well known and fascinating people over the years. One of the first was Malcolm Muggeridge, the journalist and outspoken atheist. God had chased him like 'The Hound of Heaven' until, as Malcolm himself said, 'I gave in to the unfathomable love of God'. Gerald had interviewed Malcolm at a large gathering in the Royal Albert Hall and we had been invited to visit him and his wife Kitty at their farmhouse home in Robertsbridge in Sussex. They lived very simply with no modern conveniences, certainly not a television.

After seven years at our house in Tartar Road, we needed more space so we moved to an Edwardian house in Between Streets, a few roads away.

When Paul was eight and Simon six, I developed all the tell-tale signs of another pregnancy and made an appointment with our GP.

'I think I'm expecting a baby,' I said.

'Would you like it terminated?'

I was absolutely shocked. I went home in a daze.

I asked a friend who was a midwife, 'What possible reason could two doctors give for me to have an abortion? I'm healthy, with two healthy children, happily married and no major financial problems.'

She told me they would cite mental health problems. In other words, I had not planned to have another baby.

Gerald, the boys and all of my friends were thrilled; not so my mum. When I told her the good news, her response was, 'Oh no.'

Although feeling very sick again, I was looking forward to our new baby's arrival. People kept saying, 'I expect you are hoping for a girl this time'! As it turned out, Jonathan's birth was traumatic. He had opened his bowels a few days before, a sure sign of distress, and the monitors put on him kept breaking down. By the time he was born (a whopping 8lbs 15oz), we were just so grateful he was OK.

Right from the beginning Jonathan, meaning 'Gift from God', seemed very alert. Visitors peering into his crib during the first week of his life commented, 'Goodness, he looks as if he understands what we are saying.' We always knew he would do well in finance.

After receiving his Christmas presents on Christmas Day he would sell them to his friends on Boxing Day. Later, when he was about eight, he would go to the golf course, pick up balls that players had just lost, and sell them back to them.

We impressed on each of our (very different) sons that they should be their own men. With a church leader as a father there is sometimes the pressure to behave perfectly, and follow in his footsteps – not so our boys! We've had our fair share of 'incidents' over the years. Once, when Gerald and I were out, Paul – who had just got his provisional licence at that time – thought he would practise reversing and so on in our courtyard. He managed to put *my* lovely car into the wrong gear; the car had jumped over the low wall, and crashed. When Gerald and I got there, it was hanging from the raised courtyard, its bonnet resting on the shed below. We also went through a very bad patch with Simon, when he was seventeen. He had bought a new car with a loan. Whilst taking a friend out for a drive, he crashed it into another car. When the paramedics arrived, they thought Simon was dead – he had broken ribs, was unconscious and the car door had been forced into his side, creating a huge gash and breaking his pelvis. What followed were several years of stress for us all. Simon's health, financial and legal problems were a constant worry. Simon recovered but did not settle back into his landscape gardening job and eventually went to live in Germany for a year.

We saw less and less of Mum and Dad during the years the boys were growing up. Occasionally I would invite Mum over for the day but she showed very little interest in us or the children. Dad we rarely saw.

When Jonathan was a few months old I wrote to Mum inviting her to visit on a certain date. It was during the school holidays so I thought it would be nice for her to see all the boys. Gerald had been invited to speak at a week's camp in the West Country and we suddenly received an invitation for the boys and me to join him there. I wrote to Mum explaining the situation and suggested another date; I knew she would not mind. We had a wonderful week there and returned home very happy and rested.

Gerald and I were sitting in bed the next morning with cups of coffee, opening our mail.

Mrs Coates,

At last I have been proved right, you are a mean nasty person. I was not surprised to discover you had invited your mother to come and visit and then intentionally left her standing on the door step. We never want to see you or your family ever again. Do not come to our house or make any contact with us.

A.J. Ayling

'What?' I started to laugh; I could not understand what this was all about. I read it again and then realised it was no laughing matter. My father was cutting me off completely.

After that, I was in a state of shock; it was as if there had been a death in the family. After all, although we were not close they *were* my mother and father.

I had to think this through and asked a friend, Anne Ball, to drive me to the Sheepleas, a beauty spot nearby. Here, I thought about everything, whilst Anne pushed Jonathan in his buggy. I began to realise that because of the guilt Dad felt about the past, he had to have someone to blame – and that was me. He had been waiting for an opportunity to get me out of his life and at last he had found it.

Apparently there had been a postal strike and my letter to Mum, changing the date, had not arrived until the morning she left to catch the bus. Dad had opened the letter and was furious.

I wrote to Mum, explaining what had happened. She quite understood the situation and was not particularly upset. She hadn't known anything about the letter Dad wrote to me. But she said I should not contact her; she would ring me when she could. Gerald wrote to Dad, hoping he would understand the true situation and saying that if he would write an apology we would forget the whole thing. Of course, he did not, and we never saw him again.

Endnote

[1] See Acts chapter 2.

8

Forgiveness

I grieved for my 'lost family' for about three months; it was if they had all died and I had been orphaned. Actually, this wasn't the case, as I did see Mum occasionally, when she contacted me, but it was very strained. She was obviously scared that Dad would find out.

Then, after nearly four years, a period of seven months had gone by when I had not heard from Mum. I rang my brother to ask if she was unwell. I had already decided that if I heard from Vic that Mum was ill I would visit, regardless of Dad's wishes. Apparently she was fine but a week or so later he phoned back.

'I've got some news for you. Dad has died. He's been suffering from stomach cancer and died at home last night. Could you go to see Mum?'

Shocked, I drove over to the house I had not been in for four years. Mum tearfully welcomed me. Apparently, she had wanted to contact me but Dad had forbidden it. He even said, 'If you leave that woman any money in your will, I will come back and haunt you.'

Gerald and I attended his funeral. It was a miserable affair. Dad had cursed God to the end. He had very few friends, and the people present attended for Mum's sake, not his. Three of his grandchildren had no relationship with him. What a sad and wasted life.

I could not grieve for Dad; I had already gone through that process. Mum was at last released from his grip, and we began to form a closer relationship. She enjoyed the times we spent driving in the countryside and, for the first time, began to talk about her early years. It was still too painful to look back on her married life.

Mum was born Margery Eileen Anscombe near Croydon in 1918. Her mother, Emily Lily Wilkins, had gone into service at Selsdon Park, a large mansion that is now a hotel, where she met Tom Anscombe. He was much older than her, had been married before and had three children. When Mum asked why she had married an old man, her mother replied, 'So he wouldn't live long.' I did not really understand this comment as Granny always seemed a warm, caring person to me – and surely she would not have wanted the trauma of bringing up a child on her own in those difficult days?

The early years of Mum's life were spent at Selsdon Park; she loved the gardens there and soon developed a passion for animals. I think the unconditional love the animals gave her was the only affection she received. 'Dad was a grumpy old man,' she told me, 'and my mother was too busy working to give me much attention.' When Tom became too unwell to support them, my granny worked in different large houses as a housekeeper. Her accommodation did not include room for a child so my mum was farmed out to different relations – Granny came from a large family, so uncles and aunts were paid to look after her daughter. Some were kinder than others, and in some homes Mum was very lonely and unhappy. She was a solitary child and found it hard to make friends at all the new schools she had to move to (thirteen different schools in six years!). Like many working class girls of that era, Mum left school early and started work. One of her first jobs was as a live-in nanny to a small baby; the conditions were so bad she ran (or rather, cycled) away.

During her teens, she had a boyfriend; his mother owned a tearoom in Selsdon and always made her feel welcome. I am not sure what happened to finish the romance but when she was twenty-one she got married – not to the tearoom owner's son but to her first cousin, Arthur James Ayling. Arthur and Mum's mothers were sisters and Dad's parents were the only aunt and uncle she had not lived with. Arthur was ten years older, seemed very grown up and stable and, as Mum said, 'He swept me off my feet.' Although their marriage was not a happy one, I think there must have been some romance at the beginning; Mum had nearly black hair she grew to her waist and wore in thick plaits. When they were cut off, she kept them wrapped in a drawer. When Dad died, they were placed in his coffin as he'd requested.

Dad's mother, Esther, or Ettie as she was known, trained as a cook, a very valued servant in the big houses of that day. She married Arthur Henry Ayling – an alcoholic. My father had a miserable childhood. When the family lived in East Horsley he worked on one of the big estates in the area and, because of his job as a gamekeeper, always carried a shotgun. Payday meant a visit to the local pub where he would spend all his wages on drink before staggering home. When drunk he was very violent towards his wife and son and would often threaten to shoot them. To protect himself and his mother, Dad would go to bed with a loaded gun at the ready.

Apparently, Dad was a very bright boy, excelling at maths, but because of his father's drinking he was

forced to leave school at thirteen and start work as a carpenter. He never forgave his father for the life he had
and although later he bought his parents their bungalow, he was very cruel to them in their old age. After
they both died, he took every piece of furniture and
every possession from the house and burnt it all on a
huge bonfire in the garden.

With God's help I had been able to forgive Mum and
Dad – Dad for his cruelty and Mum for not protecting
me.

It had not been easy for many years; if I was reminded of Dad, I would experience a terrible churning in
my stomach. Frankly, I knew as a Christian I should be
able to forgive but could not manage it. Then, one Easter,
Gerald and I were both speakers at the Christian event,
Spring Harvest. In the Big Top, thousands had gathered
to hear the speaker, Eric Delve. The subject that night
was 'Forgiveness' and, at the end, he asked people to
stand if they needed the power to forgive. I knew God
was speaking to me. I had to stand, and I was very tearful. Gerald, Jim Graham, another minister, and his wife
prayed with me. Jim gave me some advice which helped
greatly and I have passed it on to others: Jesus died that
we might receive forgiveness and, with his Spirit, we
can forgive others. Jim suggested that when I felt that
bitterness and anger I should pray, 'God, in your
strength and with your Spirit, I forgive (Dad) as you
have forgiven me.'

After a few months of this happening, I began to feel
a real compassion for my father and mother and an
understanding of their lives and how God saw them. I
realised that even if my father, when he was alive, did
not want to receive my forgiveness, I could still make a
difference with my attitude towards my mother.

Another thing I had found very difficult was singing hymns to God 'our Father'. I loved Jesus as my Lord and Saviour and knew the Holy Spirit as a wonderful influence and comforter but . . . God as a *Father*? My experience of a father was not a good, positive one. But I discovered that God was a *loving* Father to me. He took care of me, provided for me, lovingly disciplined me and wanted me to be the person I was created to be.

And so, I was able to live in freedom. I had learned that being able to forgive doesn't just affect the one who's forgiven; the greatest gift is to the one who forgives.

Gerald and I were happy living in Between Streets in Cobham; our sons were growing up and attending local schools. Gerald used the front room as an office and had a part-time secretary. He still travelled a lot, but our income was more stable and suited to the responsibilities he had. Our church was thriving. Cobham Christian Fellowship was no longer a suitable name, as many people now lived outside of Cobham. After much debate, the name was changed to 'Pioneer People'; other like-minded groups across Britain and overseas had wanted to connect with Gerald and be part of what we were doing, so the whole network of churches was called Pioneer.

This was an exciting time: many initiatives were to come out of Pioneer and other similar networks over the next few years that would influence thousands of people worldwide. And we made some interesting contacts.

At a Christian event in London, while queuing for food, we got chatting to Cliff Richard. We discovered he lived in nearby Weybridge and that we had many friends in common, and so began a lasting friendship. I have many happy memories of times spent with Cliff. He would host a fancy-dress party every summer in his beautiful garden on St George's Hill. Neighbours and friends with show business, tennis and church connections were invited. One particular year the theme was 'Tramps' and, as Gerald was booked to be in America on that date, I took Paul as my escort. Hair unwashed for several days, no make-up and my glasses held together with sticking plasters, I dressed for the occasion with black plimsolls, striped red and white socks, a baggy skirt, ill-fitting blouse and cardigan. Two full plastic carrier bags completed the picture. Midway through the evening, Gerald called from America.

'Sorry I can't be with you,' he said to Cliff, 'but I hope you're having a great evening.'

'I'm not sure this was a good idea,' Cliff told him, 'but Anona looks absolutely amazing.' How ironic – when I am looking my very worst I get the best ever compliment from Sir Cliff Richard!

Around the time we first met Cliff, we also got to know a married couple, Norman Miller and Sheila Walsh. They came to visit for a few weeks, and stayed for seven years! Sheila was becoming well known as a gospel singer and was on the TV programme *The Rock Gospel Show*, co-presenting with Alvin Stardust. Norman managed Sheila and worked with other artists promoting tours and concerts. Gerald and he initiated and produced a great Christian music event at Wembley Arena called 'The Banquet'.

Eventually, it was time for Norman and Sheila to buy their own property. Although they were away touring for several months of the year we looked on them as family and enjoyed the time they spent at home with us. So Gerald and I were surprised but pleased when they suggested we should buy a new house together.

We soon found the perfect one. Clive House in Esher was a beautiful Georgian property with plenty of room for two families and guests, with offices for Gerald, Norman, and Pioneer. Actually, many interesting people had lived there over the years. One was Sir Alfred Wills, the presiding judge who had sentenced Oscar Wilde to prison. One evening, Oscar Wilde's grandson, Merlin Holland, came to visit us and was intrigued to see the home of the man so involved in his grandfather's sad life. The next day we received this note

Dear Gerald and Anona,
What a fascinating evening it was and very little to do with Oscar. I find your own lives far more interesting than the now well-trodden path of Oscar's naughtiness.
Kind Regards
Merlin Holland

I was very settled, happy in our lovely home with Gerald, my sons and Norman and Sheila, fulfilled in my job as a doctor's receptionist at Esher Green Surgery and in the various roles I had in our church. My early difficult years seemed a long way away. God had blessed me and healed me of many of the hurts from the past.

And then, I had that phone call from Amanda, telling me she was sure Mum was not my real mother. It got me thinking, but I wasn't really sure I wanted to 'go there'. In truth, I had suspected all along, deep down, that something was not 'right' but was unsure whether I wanted to pursue the matter now. After speaking with Amanda, I began to look back for the first time in many years, thinking in depth about the bad experiences I'd had. I recognised the healing I'd received but I also knew there was still a hole of 'not knowing' within me.

I knew I had to discover the truth.

9

The Real Me

Being one of those people who enjoy detective stories, I am the annoying person who always knows who did it at the beginning of the film and tells everyone else. I set about the task of detecting my own story with the same enthusiasm. Was the mother I had known really my mother?

The first step was to apply for my birth certificate – a full one, not the short copy I had, that just stated

Name: Anona Joan Ayling
Sex: Female
Date of Birth: Third December 1947
Place of Birth: England

I had applied for this when I was about to be married. I'd asked Mum for my birth certificate but she'd said she had lost it. I'd thought that was rather strange but accepted that it was one of the many odd things which happened in our house. I found out later that if I *had* applied for a full copy at that time my future may have been very different.

After a few days I received a reply.

Dear Mrs Coates,

With reference to your recent application I regret I am unable to find an entry which agrees with the particulars you have supplied. Can you advise me whether the particulars shown in your application have changed in any way since that person was born i.e. perhaps as a result of a change in name, fostering, adoption etc.?

Of course I wrote back at once saying, 'Yes, there is a possibility of fostering or adoption.'

At this point I started to keep a record of what was happening and how I felt; these are my jottings a few days later

What a strange few days it has been. At last I've proved something I suspected from way back when I was a child and life did not seem to make sense. I am adopted.

When I first saw the adoption certificate, I felt I was reading about someone else, some other child. Even the setting was surreal. I was sitting in our car, in a traffic jam in Trafalgar Square, London at midnight. Gerald was with me wearing a Hawaiian shirt and I was wearing a grass skirt with a necklace of flowers around my neck. We had just left the fortieth birthday party of our friend Peter Meadows and . . . the theme had been *Hawaii Five-0*.

Gerald had left early that morning for a church conference and had taken the mail with him. Opening it during the lunch break, he realised he needed to speak to me alone.

'How would you feel if you did discover you were adopted?' he asked.

'Relieved,' I answered. So he handed me the certificate.

At first, I thought it was my birth certificate; it looked similar and had my name, my parents' names and their details and then I noticed it was headed 'Adoption

Certificate' and stated that I had been adopted on 15 July 1948 when I was seven months old.

The strongest feeling I've had since finding out is a sense of freedom. Who my natural parents are does not concern me at the moment. I feel free of all ties and responsibilities; I will be able to choose how I relate to my adoptive family which now only consists of Mum, Vic and Win, who is Mum's cousin and my godmother. I am who I am now, Gerald's wife. Mother to Paul, Simon and Jonathan, a friend and colleague of many. It's as if I have no history, a little bit like losing your memory but having people around you who know you for who you are now.

I walked around in a daze and enjoyed that sense of freedom for a couple of weeks. Then curiosity got the better of me and I started my search for the 'real me'.

The next step was to visit the Family Record Centre. At that time, it was housed in St Catherine's House in London. A friend, Dave Jupp, who was experienced in family history research, came with me. I was glad he did; it was a daunting place unless you knew the ropes, bustling with men in suits and many people like me, searching for themselves. The atmosphere was like a library as we lifted the vast volumes from shelves and found a space to lay them out to look through.

The books were arranged in yearly quarters so we found 'October, November, and December 1947' and Dave suggested looking for any connections I could think of. So we looked up relations' names first. But there were no clues there. Next, we checked my parents' marriage and my brother's birth – all accurate. Then, starting at 'A', we looked at records of births for that quarter, but found that this was taking forever and we did not really know what to look for. We finished at 'G' with arms, legs and backs aching. We had found four

Anonas but they all had married parents, and several Joans, all born in the north of England. As Dave said, we were looking for a needle in a haystack. We even looked up Jones as a surname; Dave told me new parents often give a variation of the child's original name in their new one.

Rather despondently, I collected a form so that I could officially apply for my original birth certificate. For some reason, I did not really want to go down that route, so I decided I would go and visit Mum first, to find out if she would be willing to tell me the truth.

My driving was very erratic on the journey from Esher to Effingham. I suddenly thought, 'If the police pull me over, I'll have to say, "I'm on my way to find out who I am!"'

Mum must have wondered why I was visiting in the evening – we only saw one another when I invited her out for the day – but she offered me tea and we sat down in the kitchen.

Before I lost my nerve I blurted out, 'Well, I've come to see you for a reason, Mum. I've just discovered I was adopted.'

Mum looked shocked. 'You're not upset, then?' she ventured.

'No,' I said, 'I'm relieved Dad wasn't my father.'

Immediately, I knew she understood what I meant; I had been praying she would be open about the past and she was. For the first time, we talked about our family life and how miserable we had been.

'I would have told you that you were adopted when you were in your teens,' she said, 'but your life was hell and I thought you would walk out the door. I felt responsible for you.'

'Dad was crueller to me than to you and Vic,' I said, 'don't tell me I imagined that.'

'No,' said Mum. 'He was.' Then, she added, 'Would you like to know why we adopted you?'

It was as if large doors were opening in front of me and, at last, I would be able to see the past. And this was what my mother told me.

When she and Dad married, Dad said, as they were first cousins, they would not be able to have children 'in case there's something the matter with them'. During the Second World War, many evacuees came out of the East End of London to stay in Effingham. I remembered hearing stories of them, how dirty they were with their hair full of nits. But Mum enjoyed looking after the children billeted at their house and even had a baby staying for about six months. This made her long for a baby of her own. After the war, there was no shortage of babies waiting for adoption and Mum managed to persuade Dad that they could adopt. He seemed to have had very little to do with it, other than to sign the forms. My granny, Mum's mother, was the person who supported her and went with her to the Adoption Society in Baker Street to collect a baby girl. It had to be a girl as Dad did not want the family name to be passed on through someone who was not of the same blood.

Mum took the baby to the local GP for a check-up as she had been advised, but came home in shock. The doctor had told her to return the baby – her tongue stuck out too much, she would be mentally backward. It must have been quite traumatic to take the little girl back, but a few weeks later a letter arrived.

We have another baby girl for you.

So back to London went Mum and Granny, where I was handed over, apparently about two months old, obviously well-dressed and cared for.

I was trying to take all of this in, when Mum asked, 'Would you like to find your real mother?'

'Yes,' I stuttered, 'if you'd be happy about it.'

'All I know is that your name was Carol Jones. You were born in Shropshire and your father was in the Forces and well-connected.'

So Dave had been right. I *was* a Jones – possibly my middle name was Joan because of that.

I was very grateful to Mum for being so open and supportive. She was obviously very relieved and even excited about me finding my natural mother.

On Tuesday 5 November 1991, armed with my original name, I returned to St Catherine's House. My good friend Joan Livingstone came with me. This was much easier; we soon found a Carol Jones born in December in Wellington, Shropshire and applied for the birth certificate. By the next Saturday, the certificate arrived. Sitting in bed having an early morning cup of tea, my hands were trembling as I opened the envelope. And so I found out the following details – Carol Jones, born 3 December 1947 at the Priory Nursing Home, Wellington in the County of Salop (the old name for Shropshire), father unknown, but mother Christine Jones. She was a shorthand typist. Address: 5 Squarefield Terrace, Moor Lane, Woodford in Cheshire.

It is hard to describe how I felt reading this. I could not imagine myself as this little baby Carol and it was even harder to picture my mother 'Christine'. Perhaps she was young when she had got pregnant and, as her home address was quite a distance from where I had been born, maybe she had been sent away in disgrace. I had the same surname as her but as my father was 'unknown' they probably weren't married. I thought, 'It must have been tough being an unmarried mother in those days.'

Strangely, it did not bother me to find out that I was probably illegitimate. What did amaze me was that Dad had never let it slip out, although, during outbursts when he would call me every name he could think of, he would often call me a bastard. However, I think that was only in the general insulting way.

I believe he never told me and had destroyed all the paperwork because all the time I thought I was his child he had a hold on me. I think that if I had known I would, as Mum said, have walked out the door.

As I had read that there were over five hundred thousand Joneses in the UK, this was not going to be easy. Still, it had to be done. So, on Monday 11 November 1991, I sat in the alcove at home with a note pad at the ready and started making phone calls.

I started with the Priory Nursing Home in Wellington. A pleasant-sounding lady answered the phone. I briefly explained that I had been born there in 1947, and did they keep any records?

Sadly, she told me that it was now a residential home for the elderly and the one person that would have remembered and known where the records were had died a few months ago. So, no joy there.

My next call was to Stockport council offices. I had discovered that Woodford was in that area.

'I'm doing some family research,' I said, 'and wondered if the address 5 Squarefield Terrace, Moor Lane in Woodford still exists?'

The man I spoke to said he would investigate and ring me back. After thirty minutes the phone rang. The nearest he could find was a house called Squarefield in that area.

'Would you like the name of the people living there?' he asked.

Dad with my grandparents Arthur and Ettie at their bungalow.

Probably the first photo of me with Mum and her mother Lily.

Mum, Dad, Vic and me on a windswept pier at Ryde, Isle of Wight.

Just engaged and looking very serious. Gerald and me on the roof garden at Harvey's department store in Guildford.

Gerald, me, Simon aged four and Paul aged six in front of our first home, 41 Tartar Road, Cobham.

Jonathan during his skateboarding years.

Christine on her wedding day, being given away by her father.

Our first meeting. Nick, Kathryn, me and Christine.

Werner aged 17, taken in Poland four weeks after he was called up.

Werner when a POW in Maryland, USA.

Photo taken by Christine in 1946. At the POW camp in Woodford. Ernst, Werner and a friend.

The day we met. Werner and me in his garden in Germany.

Gerald and me with Cliff at the World Youth Day in Bonn, Germany.

Paul and Lisa's wedding in our garden. With our new granddaughter Lola.

Simon, looking sun-tanned as usual.

Jonathan and his lovely fiancée Joanna.

'Yes, please,' I said.

It was very easy to get their phone number from Directory Enquiries but I felt very nervous about ringing them. I did not think they would be relations but how would they feel about a strange woman bothering them? After praying that the call would be well received, and with my heart in my mouth, I dialled their number.

'Hello, Gillian here.'

I explained again how I was doing some family research and wondered if a family called Jones had lived in their house forty-three years ago. Gillian said that it had not been built that long, but could she help?

'I must be honest with you,' I replied. 'I've just discovered I was adopted as a baby and I'm looking for my natural family, so I must be very careful not to cause problems for them.'

Gillian understood completely. She was sure that she knew a Mrs Jones who lived nearby in Moor Lane, where Squarefield Terrace had been. After looking in the telephone directory, she said, 'Yes, a Mrs A.E. Jones lives there,' and added that she was sure this lady had a daughter . . . If I could give her a few days, she said, she could make some discreet enquiries and get back to me.

Gill, as I now called her, rang the following Saturday. She had discovered that Mrs Jones was not the person she'd first thought; instead, she was a white-haired lady, very liked and respected in the area. Gill had asked her sister who Mrs Jones's daughter was.

'Oh,' said Gill's sister. 'Christine.'

10

My New Family

A few days before this, at a church meeting, we had been
encouraged to turn to two or three other people and ask
for prayer for a specific need. My request was that on
my birthday, 3 December 1991, I would receive a card
from my natural mother. Two close friends, Robyn and
Lynne, who knew the whole story, prayed for me.

I could not believe it; already, after only a week, a few
phone calls and some wonderfully helpful people, I had
my natural mother's details. I was so grateful to God.

Still, I had read many horror stories of people who
had found out who their birth parents were and had just
arrived on the doorstep, announcing, 'I am your child.'
The shock probably made it very hard for the parent to
cope, and unsurprisingly, rejection was the most common response.

I was prepared for rejection but felt the easier it was
made for my mother, the more likely we were of a successful reunion. Gill's sister had supplied Christine's
address and phone number – her married name was
Edge and she only lived a mile or so away from her
mother. However, not knowing if her husband or maybe
children knew about me, I did not want to make life difficult for her.

How to make contact in a gentle way?

Gerald remembered a minister of a church in Runcorn, not too far away. Perhaps he would be happy to be a go-between? I phoned John and explained the situation. We decided he would phone Christine, say who he was and explain he was phoning for a lady who lived in Surrey and believed she was Christine's daughter. If anyone else answered the phone, he would put the receiver down and try later.

When he passed on the message, Christine's response was, 'Oh, Carol! I've never forgotten her. I didn't want to give her away but my parents made me. I always think of her on her birthday and look at women in the street and wonder, is that her?'

She said she would have to break the news to her son and daughter; her husband had known about me but had died eighteen months before. Her mother had never referred to the incident since the adoption forty-three years ago.

A few days later, John received a call. Christine had spoken to her children, Kathryn and Nicholas. Apparently, they had met at Kathryn's house.

'I want to tell you something,' Christine had said. 'You have an older sister!'

After she had explained, they'd both hugged her.

'You're still our mum and we love you!'

And Kathryn had said that she'd always wanted an older sister.

John then told me that Christine would like us to correspond and could I write first?

But what do you write to your closest relative, who you do not know? I explained how I'd recently discovered I'd been adopted and my journey to find her. Then about my husband and three sons, how I was working as a doctor's receptionist and, as a committed Christian, was very involved in the church – also that I had no bad feelings about the adoption and, if it was possible, I would love to meet her one day.

On my birthday, Gerald handed me the mail saying, 'Here's a card from your mum and here's another card from your mum.'

I was so moved to receive that card. I remembered that specific prayer, prayed by Robyn and Lynne. What an answer!

Next, a letter arrived with a photo of the family. I thought I could see some resemblance between me and Christine and her mother – Gran Jones, as I called her. Kathryn and Nicholas were very like their father, Dennis. It transpired that Christine and Dennis had met in 1951 and married two years later. She had told Dennis about me on their fourth date; I was so glad that he had known. They even thought they would look for me when he had retired from the railway company but sadly he had become ill and died before that was possible.

Kathryn was born in 1959 and Nick in 1962. They both left home quite early, Kathryn to go to Catering College where she met her first husband. She had two daughters, Charlotte and Rebecca. I found out that Rebecca's birthday was the day before mine. Christine later told me that this 'made me happy but sad'. Nick went into the army at sixteen; Christine had to be persuaded to give her permission. He had served in Northern Ireland and was injured in the face by a missile thrown at his armoured vehicle. He had been married to Jacqui for two years.

I discovered I also had a family in America. Kathleen, Christine's elder sister, had married her boyfriend and moved to Seattle. My two cousins were Janet, an architect married to Mike with two children, and Susan.

Christine had contacted them about me and I received a lovely card welcoming me to the family – belatedly!

Christine did not want her mother to find out that I had made contact. She was eighty-three and Christine thought perhaps she would be upset to have the past dragged up again.

I was thrilled to discover that Christine was also a believer. She was a member of Grove Lane Baptist Church in Cheadle Hulme and loved attending more charismatic meetings rather like our church held. She had heard of Gerald and had planned to go with friends to a meeting at the Free Trade Hall in Manchester where he was speaking but Dennis had been unwell and she'd had to drop out. I think she was more thrilled to discover that Gerald was her son-in-law than I was her daughter!

Of course, while all this was happening, I was getting on with my normal life. My colleagues at the doctor's surgery were very supportive and interested in my hunt for my family. I shared a little of my past, and particularly my childhood, with a few.

One friend said, 'How is it, after all you've been through, you are so normal and together?'

'It's only the grace of God,' I replied. Her eyes filled with tears.

I'd kept my creative side going by dressing windows for some local shops. One was Oasis, the book and card shop our church ran in Cobham. Keep Fit and Art classes gave me some time for myself. Then there was the usual 'stuff' of life – the shopping, washing, ironing, cooking, cleaning; Clive House was a big place to keep going. Our sons took it in turns to clean the offices in the stable block and a good friend, Coral Kay, helped me with the housework. Some men from the church came over once a month to garden so Gerald could be freed up for the work he was doing.

We seemed to do a lot of entertaining. My diary of that time is full of having friends for meals or going out for meals with others. We also held a New Year's Eve party, inviting friends from many different backgrounds. This proved to be a great success and became a tradition for many years.

At that time, Gerald and I had become guardians for a boy from Malaysia. I had picked up a parish magazine from St Andrew's Church in Cobham; it contained an appeal for a family to host a pupil from the Yehudi Menuhin School in nearby Stoke D'Abernon for the school holidays. The host family would need a piano and have to be able to allow four hours' piano practice every day. We had the piano and the room so I applied to the headmaster, Nicholas Chisholm. Bobby Chen, his parents and younger brother Percy were brought to see us by his mentor, the man who had discovered Bobby's amazing musical gift while in Malaysia. When Gerald opened the front door, he was shocked. The mentor was Geoffrey Smith; he had been the youth leader at the Gospel Hall in Cobham when Gerald had been a lad.

Bobby's grandmother was a devout Christian and had prayed that Bobby would stay with a church family in England, hence the advert in the parish magazine. Bobby was only eleven, a little round-faced boy. It was not easy for him to be away from his family in a strange country with all the cultural differences.

After doing so well at the Yehudi Menuhin School, he spent four years at the Royal Academy of Music, graduating with First Class Honours. Bobby was the first Malaysian pianist to be invited to play at the Concert Hall at the Petronas Twin Towers in Kuala Lumpur. But, as well as being a world-class concert pianist, Bobby has grown into a lovely young man. He always asks us to any local concerts and it was after a wonderful debut at Wigmore Hall in London that he hugged us and thanked us for all our care. We were so proud of him and pleased we had played a small part in his life.

As well as all this, church activities, some public speaking and a little writing also kept me busy. My life was very varied and satisfying. However, my priority was to get to know my new family.

On the morning of Sunday 15 December 1991, Gerald and I were having breakfast when the phone rang. I saw the surprise on his face. It was Christine! Apparently, she had phoned on Friday night, we were out and Jonathan had forgotten to tell us.

I listened to them chatting and then, with my heart thumping, spoke to my mother for the first time. It was strange to hear her Cheshire accent; she later asked me if I had taken elocution lessons as I sounded so posh! We were both rather nervous but soon were feeling more at ease. One new thing she mentioned was that her mother worked in a dress shop during the war – and also dressed the windows.

We spoke about twice a week after that first time and Christine told me a little more about the past. She was only sixteen when she'd discovered she was pregnant. Her father wanted her to stay at home but her mother arranged for her to stay with her Aunty Gladys near Wellington in Shropshire until I was born. After two weeks she returned home, then aged seventeen. Once home, nothing was said about the pregnancy, birth or coming adoption. I think it must have been so hard not to talk over what had happened. On Christmas Day, she sat with her family around the table, and they were all crying. Then her father could stand it no longer, and went upstairs.

I later discovered that some neighbours had offered to adopt me but Christine's parents thought it would be difficult with me growing up next door.

Although nowadays to send a young girl away from home seems very heartless it was the usual thing to do in that era. Her mother thought that she would be stigmatised as an unmarried mother and would certainly never find a decent husband. Any prospect of a normal family life and security in the future would be remote. Still, to suddenly disappear for six months had to be explained, so people were told she was going away to have an operation on an eye which had always had problems. I don't think many people believed this excuse as the eye was just the same when she returned.

As time went on and we talked more, I realised that being sent away from home left her feeling totally rejected by the family she had always felt so safe with and loved by. This was even more traumatic than not having my father to support her, giving birth to me and leaving me with the aunt to be adopted.

Until that point, I had not thought much about my father.

When Christine phoned me that Sunday morning, she said to Gerald, 'I will never be able to tell Anona who her father is.'

He made light of it and suggested that it was something we could discuss in the future. But I made a decision then not to ask her about my real father. If she ever felt she could tell me about him, then that would be fine, but I wouldn't push her.

We were all feeling it would now be good to meet. I had spoken to Kathryn on the phone and sent Christmas cards but now it was time to see my family face to face.

It was decided we would meet at a halfway point. Kathryn's husband suggested a hotel, the Post House in Great Barr near Birmingham. Gerald and I would drive up together and Christine, Kathryn and Nick would make their way down to meet us there.

I spent quite a while gathering old photos of myself as a baby and small child and then made copies (which was not so easy without negatives in 1992). With other photos of our wedding, my sons and more up-to-date ones of us all, I put together an album of the lost years for Christine.

To be meeting my nearest blood relations for the first time at the age of forty-four was both exciting and nerve-racking. As we drove up the motorway, I kept saying to Gerald, 'This is the strangest day of my life!'

Sitting in a coffee lounge at the hotel, Gerald and I recognised them as soon as they walked in. Although I did not think I had the same features as Christine, we had many characteristics that were the same. The way we sat, waved our hands around, all the things Amanda saw were missing when she met my adoptive mother on that day four months previously.

'You're so big!' commented my mother.

Yes, I'd grown quite a lot in the last forty-four years.

Kathryn and I laughed when we looked at one another. We were both wearing the same kind of clothes and jewellery – but in different colours, because our colouring was different.

After hugs and kisses, we talked non-stop through coffee, then lunch, just getting to know one another, beginning to feel more comfortable. Kathryn and Nick seemed very much at ease and Christine said she would now tell her mother that I had made contact.

I think we all returned home happy – but exhausted.

11

The Discovery

Christine came to stay with us in February. It must have been quite an experience for her, travelling by train down from Stockport to Watford, where I collected her and drove her round the M25 to Esher. We talked for hours about our lives and looked through piles of photo albums. I felt we were more like sisters than mother and daughter. I'd found her at just the right time; with Dennis gone she'd felt lonely. Now, suddenly she had new people and new interests in her life, although of course it brought back all the unhappy memories of the past.

Simon was still living in Germany but she met Paul and Jonathan and, on Jonathan's birthday, we went out for a meal at our favourite Chinese restaurant, the Good Earth, only a few steps away from our home in Esher. We also met Paul for lunch at Hampton Court Palace, where he was working in marketing, and had a private mini tour.

Next, I took Christine to visit Mum at Effingham. This was a strange visit but they seemed to get on very well. As we were leaving, Christine kissed Mum goodbye and thanked her for looking after me.

Several interesting things came out as we were talking during that visit. Christine had told her mother that I'd recently discovered I was adopted and had traced her, and that we had corresponded, spoken on the phone and then met.

'Well, that's nice,' her mother had said, 'but you won't be seeing her again, will you?'

'Oh, yes,' Christine had replied. 'I'm going to visit her and her family.'

Apparently, Gran Jones was not pleased; she must have felt when I was adopted that that would be the end of the story and no way did she want the past dug up! She had made the decision at the time and, I suppose, in her eyes, all had worked out well. Christine had also wanted to tell her childhood girlfriends about me, as they'd known she had been pregnant. But her mother had said, 'No, let's keep it in the family.' Still, for the first time since my birth, my grandmother had talked to Christine about what had happened. She had sent Aunty Gladys money to look after Christine, and then me. She had also been very annoyed to discover I had not been wearing the new outfit she had sent for my trip to London to be adopted. Later, I wondered if she was the one who had said that my father was in the Forces and well-connected.

Christine did talk to me about my father; it was as if she was working up to telling me who he was. Apparently he had not been married; at least that was what he'd said. He knew I had been born and they wrote to one another before and after the birth. In appearance, he'd been blond with fine features. She had taken a photo of him but had torn it up later; she said Adam Faith had reminded her of him. The Registrar had tried to make her put my father's name on my birth certificate but she had refused. She told me, 'He was incidental. You will have to make do with me.' That really upset me. No parent is 'incidental'; part of me was him. I cried myself to sleep that night.

Christine was also upset that day. After reading
Gerald's autobiography, *An Intelligent Fire*, and listening
to Mum, she started to realise that my adoptive home
had not been as happy as she had imagined. I determined she would never know the full story.

A few days after she returned home, I received a lovely
card thanking me for the visit. She enclosed a cheque for
me to buy a silver teapot I had admired in an antique shop
near Hampton Court. She wrote, 'This is several years of
birthday presents,' and I was very touched.

Within a week or so, my brother Nick and his wife
Jacqui had called in to visit us. Jacqui had relations on
the south coast and they were returning home; it was
lovely to see them. Then, Gerald and I celebrated our
twenty-fifth wedding anniversary in March 1992 and
our friends arranged a wonderful party in the barn at
Paul and Amanda Williams's home. All my natural family sent cards for our anniversary. So much had happened in a few short months!

Plans had also been made for Jonathan and me to go
up to Cheadle Hulme over the Easter holidays and
apparently Gran Jones was now, if not exactly happy, at
least *resigned* to me being part of their lives – and would
like to meet me on that visit. I was so glad that Jonathan
was coming with me; I had the feeling it would be a
scary event. I would meet all the family and see the area
where Christine had grown up and where I was conceived.

We were to stay at Christine's home, a three bedroom,
semi-detached house in a pleasant road in Cheadle
Hulme. I obviously did not take after her in the housework department; I have always been quite fussy and
like order. I am forever sorting out wardrobes and cupboards. The local charity shops love me; I'm always
clearing out my home of unnecessary clutter.

Christine had warned me she did as little housework as possible so I was not surprised to have the door opened by her friend who had insisted she herself would clean through the house before I arrived. Apparently it was quite a joke amongst Christine's family and friends – they all knew she would only buy clothes that did not need ironing, did the minimum of housework and cooked the easiest of meals. I found out that one day she had been burgled, and when the police arrived they were shocked.

'They've made a terrible mess of your room,' they'd said.

'Oh no,' Christine had replied, 'it was always like this. They broke into another room!' She'd had no idea if anything had been stolen.

A few years later I watched the Mike Leigh film, *Secrets and Lies*. The story is about a girl who looks for and finds her natural mother. The family was very different to mine but one similarity struck me. The mother hoarded things, just like Christine. She could not throw anything away. Even the greenhouse was full, not of plants but of household bits and pieces and clothes. Walking in Christine's garden, I noticed her greenhouse was full to overflowing with items of no use to her. These two mothers, the fictional one and the real one, had given up their babies but kept everything else . . . I wonder what a psychiatrist would make of that.

Jonathan and I were made welcome, and someone went to collect Gran Jones. She must have been very nervous, for when she arrived, she was wearing two skirts and odd shoes. I felt for her and kissed her on the cheek. As we ate the high tea (sandwiches, cake and trifle), I caught her giving me surreptitious glances, obviously trying to get the measure of me.

During the next few days, I was introduced to the wider family, Christine's school friends and people from her church. Everyone was interested in our story, thrilled I had found Christine and so pleased for us both. I think this made it easier for Gran Jones to accept me. I felt very moved when I was able to worship with Gran and Christine at their church and be introduced with no embarrassment.

One thing that happened, though, upset me a lot. Gran, Christine and I were sitting in Gran's house and I was admiring her collection of family photos.

'Yes,' she said, proudly, 'they're all my grandchildren.'

'No!' I wanted to shout. 'You've three others.'

I later wrote to Gran Jones, saying how glad I was to have met her, and that I understood how difficult the situation must have been for the family when I was born, and that I had no bad feelings towards her. Although she did not reply, I heard she told Christine she had received a lovely letter from me.

On Good Friday, we left with best wishes and many hugs and kisses. We drove across country to Skegness where we would join Gerald at Spring Harvest. Jonathan soon fell asleep in the car and I must admit I cried for a good hour, barely able to see the road ahead. Meeting everyone, being in the home my mother grew up in and hearing all the family stories had been quite traumatic. This was the family I could have lived with. But I could not really understand my feelings, because if I had lived with them, I would never have married Gerald and had my three sons. Yet, strangely, it still seemed a great loss.

Christine and I soon settled into a pattern. We would speak on the phone at least twice a week, sharing all our news. Then every few months she would come down to Esher to visit. I gradually introduced her to more friends and neighbours and sometimes I would take the two mums out for the day. They were very different and privately a little critical of one another but, for my sake, managed to get on quite well.

My adopted mum decided she would tell Vic about my adoption but feared he would be upset. She eventually plucked up the courage, though, and told him.

'Yes,' he said. 'I knew already. The neighbours told me. I wasn't sure if it was true. I decided to say nothing. If it was true I might cause trouble, and if it wasn't true I would cause trouble.'

So, everyone (but me!) seemed to know I had been adopted – relations, neighbours, even my brother Vic and my best friend, Susie. I remembered the day she'd said, 'You're adopted, you know,' and I'd just smiled, 'I wish I was.'

Mum began to blossom. No longer having to keep a big secret seemed to give her a new lease of life. She began to take more of an interest in Gerald and his travels and work, and particularly in our sons, which really pleased me. She was even freer to talk about Dad and the past. I told her how, because of God's help, I had found the strength to forgive Dad for how he had treated me. I was not sure if she understood but she was happy to come with me to the events our church put on for retired people. For the first time, she heard the gospel which had changed my life.

At this point, Christine had still not told me who my father was but continued to drop hints, so I decided to try to find out a little more.

'Was he in the Forces?' I asked.

'Yes.'

'Was he British?'

'No.'

'*No*?'

'No, though we met in Woodford.'

That gave me a big clue. She had shown me the site of an aircraft factory near the village. Apparently, during and after the war there were many American personnel based in Woodford.

'Perhaps my father was a GI,' I thought to myself. That would be very romantic! But why was his identity such a big secret? I started to daydream; perhaps he was famous and if I made contact it could ruin his career . . . Then, my stomach turned. Maybe he had raped her. That worried me, so I'd asked her if he was a bad person.

'Oh no, he was really nice.'

I was baffled.

Kathryn came with Christine on one of her visits. It felt very strange but good to be able to go shopping or just sit chatting to my own sister. I must have confided in her about my puzzlement about my father at some point, because on that visit, after dinner, when we sat down to have coffee, she turned to her mother.

'Now would be a good time for you to tell Anona about her father,' she said.

'All right.' Christine looked at me. 'Well, he was in the Forces, and I believe you think he was American.' She took a deep breath. 'He wasn't. He was German, a prisoner of war.'

12

About My Father

Just like my other mother, once Christine started to talk, it just poured out.

His name was Werner Braukmann. He had celebrated his twenty-third birthday while she knew him and she had bought him a cigarette lighter.

The prisoner of war camp was in the field just behind her house. The winter of 1946/47 was bitter with thick snow covering most of England. Sledges were used to deliver milk, and horses were used instead of motors. Schools were shut and food was in short supply. The men would march off to work in the morning, usually working on local farms, replacing men in the British army who were still in Europe. A year after the war had finished, more than four hundred thousand German POWs were still detained. Apparently many people opposed the keeping of prisoners for so long in Britain and questions were asked in parliament because it broke the rules of the Geneva Convention. But, because they were needed, they stayed.

It must have been miserable living in huts in the field but because the war had been over for a while the camp was relaxed. The prisoners were allowed free time as long as they were back by dusk. Werner played football against teams from other camps; he probably even played against Bert Trautmann, the famous German football player who, after the war, married a local girl – this was made legal in 1947. (Bert stayed in England and played for Manchester City, and in one game he continued playing with a broken neck.) Out of the 402,000 POWs held in Britain, 25,000 never went home.

Werner and his friend, Ernst, befriended Christine and her friend, Joan. They would go for long walks, and even go on the bus to the nearest cinema. A kindly guard would lend Werner his long, warm coat.

At sixteen, Christine was quite an innocent. Apparently they made love once, in the snow under a bush. Not many people know the exact moment they were conceived! I asked Christine if he had webbing between his fingers and toes like our son, Simon.

'I don't know,' she replied. 'He never took his shoes and socks off.'

Her parents were very fond of Werner, even inviting him and Ernst to spend Christmas Day 1946 at their home. This was not an uncommon occurrence. By then many people were beginning to feel sorry for the young men still away from home and, after meeting them, realised they were not unlike their own sons.

Of course, all this changed when Christine told her parents that she was pregnant. They never spoke to Werner again and Christine was packed off to Aunty Gladys. Not before she had told him she was expecting a baby, however.

Werner said, 'Can't you get rid of it?'

That was not an option. Although it was not impossible to arrange an abortion, it was still illegal at that time. Besides, neither her parents nor she would consider it. Apparently, after his initial reaction, Werner softened and said he would help all he could.

They wrote to one another over the next few months and he knew I had been born. Christine told me that after she had returned home, he wrote saying that he was being sent back to Germany and would love to meet her under the clock at Victoria Station on his way to the Boat Train. She could not afford to make the journey and her parents refused to lend her the money. Although very romantic, I think she had been watching too many films as this did not tie in with details I was to find out later.

I was not upset to discover my father was a German and not a genial GI, but was disappointed to hear he had suggested that Christine should 'get rid' of me. Thinking it over, however, I realised this was perhaps a normal reaction when first hearing such news. I was moved and grateful Christine had been able to tell me the truth. I could at last understand why it had all been such a terrible secret and why my grandparents had forced her to have me adopted. With memories of the war still fresh in everyone's mind, to have a child with enemy blood in its veins was possibly the very worst that could befall a respectable family. So, there had been no alternative. I would be taken far away, given a new name and would grow up in a home where my background would not be known. Loved and cared for by my new parents, the whole nasty incident would never be mentioned again.

By now, Sheila had been asked to host a popular American Christian television show, *The 700 Club* with Pat Robertson, and Norman was managing several bands in the States. It seemed sensible for them to move there and, obviously, they needed to take their share of the house. So, we sold Clive House and Gerald and I bought our new home in Lakeside Drive, Esher.

The moving date coincided with Gerald being away yet again at Spring Harvest for two weeks, so I organised the move myself, not without incident. We had bought a very old French chandelier from the previous owner of Clive House, and decided to take it to our new home. I asked Ian Hood, my friend Mary's husband, if he could take it down and re-hang it at Lakeside Drive. On the day of the move, I suggested Ian stood on the very solid dining-room table while he unscrewed the chandelier. He then asked Mary to be ready to take the weight, so she joined him on the table, and so did I. We were all in place as the last screw came out. The table collapsed. My son Simon found us lying on the floor surrounded by debris still hanging onto the remains of the chandelier.

My relationship with my new family continued to grow, as I got to know Nick and Jacqui and Kathryn and her husband and their children. Christine and I continued to visit one another and, in December, Paul went with me to Cheadle Hulme to meet more of the family and to celebrate, for the first time, my birthday with my natural mother, brother and sister. Gran Jones had died after a stroke, fortunately not suffering for long. I was glad we had met and she knew all was well.

Another thing that happened was that I suddenly discovered friends and acquaintances who had been adopted. I told my story to anyone who was interested and was fascinated to hear of other people's experiences. Many people asked me if I thought they should look for their birth mother. I made it clear that it was a very personal decision; they may have success and a happy ending but equally it could be very upsetting. I said, 'Do *not* look for your mother or father when you are going through a traumatic time in your life, taking exams, leaving home, getting married, going through a divorce, or if you are unwell or unstable in any way, particularly emotionally.' I felt the person would need to be as stable as possible and have lots of support, if not from family and friends then from professionals experienced in helping people through what could be one of the most life-changing events they would have, whether it turned out to be a good experience or bad.

After hearing my story, one lady in her sixties decided that she would look for her mother. She had been told she was an orphan and was adopted by a nurse from the orphanage. She was able to hire a private investigator and discovered she was not an orphan; her mother was still alive. She met her mother before she died and got to know some of her brothers and sisters. Another woman had grown up with her mother but had never known her father. She was told he was a German POW; sadly, she never managed to trace him. She got pregnant herself when in her teens and was sent to a mother-and-baby home where she was pressurised into giving up her twins. She did later find them and has an ongoing relationship with them and their children.

Every story is different – every mother who has had to give up a child and every child who has grown up wondering why.

I was still working part-time at Esher Green Surgery and, one day, the practice manager asked me for help. A patient had just lost her elderly mother and, after looking through her mother's papers, had discovered she had been adopted. Now in her sixties, the lady had decided to find out the truth and phoned to ask if there was anything in her medical records that would give a clue to her past. The records did not go back that far so the practice manager could not help. She asked me to ring the lady to see if I could advise her. I did and we chatted for ages, telling our stories, but she was already progressing well as she had gone through NORCAP, the organisation which helps adopted adults find out more about their past. She suddenly mentioned she had been adopted from the National Adoption Society in Baker Street, London.

Baker Street! That was where Mum and Granny had gone to collect me; perhaps they would have more details of my adoption.

After a few phone calls, I discovered the National Adoption Society had closed down and the file was held by Brent Council Social Services. I promptly applied to see my records and received a reply saying that I would have to have counselling before having access to them. Apparently, people have been known to attack members of their families after reading the circumstances of their adoption, so each person is assessed by a counsellor.

I made the appropriate appointment and soon was sitting in an office in Epsom talking to a very sympathetic woman. She made the mistake of asking for my story – one hour later the poor woman was in tears. Blowing her nose, she asked if I would like to see my records.

Rather apprehensively I said, 'Yes.'

A faded pink file was produced. I was surprised to see handwritten letters from the family and copies of the letters the Society had sent back. The counsellor kindly offered to make photocopies of them, and also of the application form which had been filled in by Gran Jones and signed by Christine.

I quickly scanned through it all in the office but was keen to return home where I could take my time and cope with the emotions I was feeling.

So I grasped the photocopies, went home, and began to read.

13

Letters

The first letter was from Aunty Gladys.

July 5th, 1947
Dear Sir (or Madam),
I am writing to you for advice as I need it badly; my niece, who is only sixteen years old, is going to have a baby in November. She comes from a very respectable home and needless to say her parents are broken-hearted; I am taking care of her until after the event, and I hope to be able to get the child adopted for her, so that she may have a fresh start in life after having made such a mistake to begin with.

Can you help me at all or can you send me particulars of how to set about getting the baby adopted?

Unfortunately we do not know the man who is responsible, we only know that he was an airman.

I do so hope you will be able to do something for us, as we are all so very worried as the mother to be is only a slip of a girl.

Thanking you in anticipation of an early reply.
                    Yours very sincerely,
                        G.M. Jones

She must have had a reply because she wrote again in December.

December 8th, 1947

Dear Madam,

With reference to your advice of 7.7.47 regarding the adoption of my niece's baby.

My niece gave birth to a baby girl on December 3rd. Will you please send me forms and particulars regarding the adoption of the baby? As my niece is only seventeen and is not a bad girl but an ignorant one, we are anxious to give her a new start in life.

Yours sincerely,

G.M. Jones

The photocopies of the typewritten letters from the Adoption Society were very faded; I just managed to read them.

January 15th, 1948

Dear Miss Jones,

I am pleased to tell you my Committee have agreed to help you in the adoption of your baby Carol and we have today mentioned her to a very nice family and hope very much an appointment will be made to see her here on Tuesday week, January 27th at 2 p.m. If she appeals to them when they see her, they will be prepared to take her at once on the usual trial visit of three months and it will be necessary for you to bring all her rationing documents and clothes, and a written list as to diet and routine. We will write to you again as soon as we hear definitely about this appointment.

Sincerely yours,

. . . . . .

Secretary

The next letter was from Gran Jones.

January 17th, 1948

Dear Madam,

I am writing for my daughter Christine, in reply to your letter of the 15th regarding the adoption of the baby, Carol. And to thank you on her and our behalf for helping her so much.

The baby is with my sister-in-law in Shropshire, with whom Christine stayed, and she writes that the little one is happy now and very good.

Will it be alright if she brings the baby to you for the appointment as Christine is settled down at home now and we feel it would rekindle everything we would like her to forget? Thanking you again.

> Yours sincerely,
> Doris Jones

This letter asks for my identity card, ration book and clothing coupon.

January 19th, 1948

Dear Mrs Jones,

I thank you for your letter and I am glad to know that your daughter, Christine, has settled down at home. It will be quite in order for her aunt to bring baby Carol here for the appointment on Tuesday, January 27th at 2 p.m. and will you please pass this letter on to her as it will be necessary for her to bring with baby her identity card, ration book – complete with the names and addresses of the retailers – and the extra soap permit, her clothing coupons, a parcel of all the clothes she has, a bottle of orange juice and cod liver oil, a packet of food if on a patent food, and if on National Dried Milk the book of vouchers also, her 2 p.m. feed (which we will heat) and a written list as to baby's diet and routine.

Will you please give the enclosed Memorandum form to your daughter for her to keep but she should sign and return the receipt attached at the foot as soon as possible, and may we know at the same time that this appointment for the 27th will be kept without fail.

> Sincerely yours,
>
> . . . . . .
>
> Secretary

Apparently all went well on the day. Two aunts, Gladys and Vera, actually took me to London. I imagine them in one room handing me over, perhaps feeling sad but relieved, and Mum and Granny in the other room, excited about the future but a little apprehensive as this was not the first time they had collected a baby girl from that office.

February 9th, 1948
Dear Mrs Jones,
You will be glad to know that we have received a very good report of Christine's baby; the adopters tell us how well she has settled down and that she is happy and contented. Both adopters are already very fond of baby who always has a smile for them.

   We shall be writing to you again in about one month's time and shall hope to send you more good news.

> Yours sincerely,
>
> . . . . . .
>
> Secretary

Here, Gran Jones was obviously getting concerned as she had no news for several months.

May 24th, 1948
Dear Miss Blackburne,
I am writing to ask you if the adoption of Christine's baby, Carol, has gone through, as I have only received the

one letter, regarding the baby's welfare. I was very upset as the letter came in an unsealed envelope, although it was a stamped addressed envelope which I had sent to you.

Will you please let me know about the baby? Enclosed is stamped addressed envelope.

Yours sincerely,
Doris E. Jones

I seemed to remember Mum saying that they only had a couple of visits to check all was well. From photos of that time, I certainly looked healthy and very chubby, a positive thing in the post-war years.

May 28th, 1948
Dear Mrs Jones,
I thank you for your letter and I am very sorry to hear that unfortunately our last letter of March 19th, sent to your same address, did not reach you. I am glad to let you know at once that baby is progressing extremely well. She goes to the clinic regularly and the doctor considers she is a very forward bright baby. Her adopters have become very fond of her.

The legal procedure through the court takes a little time and we are expecting to receive certain legal forms and we shall be writing to you with regard to these.

I note what you say about the unsealed envelope; I know our postal clerk is very careful but we do find that some of the gum on envelopes these days is extremely poor.

Yours sincerely,
. . . . . .
Secretary

It was not until October that the final letter was received.

October 13th, 1948

Dear Miss Jones,

You will be glad to know that the Legal Order has been granted for the adoption of your little girl and she has been now entered in her new name. As we have always told you, little Carol is in an excellent home where she is receiving much love and good care and you now have no further cause for anxiety as to her future.

My Committee wish me to explain that our work is supported entirely by voluntary contributions and they feel that when a mother has been relieved of much worry and expense she will wish to contribute something towards helping other children placed in similar circumstances. It costs about £8 to arrange each adoption and so if you are able to send us something towards this we should much appreciate it.

Yours sincerely,

. . . . . .

Secretary

The £8 was never sent.

I was transported back in time as I read the letters and felt very emotional. How hard it must have been for everyone. I could also picture myself, little Carol. Do events that happen when you are a tiny baby have any lasting effect? I'm not sure. I do know the rejection I felt in later life came from the experiences in my adoptive home.

Reading through the official application form was very interesting. All the normal questions had been answered – names, dates and addresses. My father had been put down as 'unknown' but British and in the RAF. The full account of the details was fascinating reading but completely untrue.

My daughter, Christine, was seventeen years old on September 1st. It came as a great shock to us when we knew she was pregnant, as we did not know she had been associating with anyone. On close questioning we discovered that she had only met the man responsible once, as he did not keep the next appointment.

Owing to the fact that she did not even know his name, or where he came from, we could not do anything about it. The only thing she did know was that he was an English boy in the RAF.

If we had known who he was, we could not have allowed her to marry as she is such a child in her ways as well as her age.

Our home is at Woodford, Cheshire, and as we are very well known there and in the surrounding districts, we decided that Christine should come to her aunties until it was all over, so that when everything was settled she should have a fresh start in life. That being the chief reason why we would like to get the baby adopted.

> Doris Jones
> (Mother)

I pictured Christine sitting at the kitchen table reluctantly writing

> I am quite willing to have my baby adopted.
> Christine Jones
> 23-12-47

Two days before Christmas.

Why was such a big lie told? From what I had heard of Gran Jones, she had been a very upright and honest person. Perhaps she thought that no one would want to adopt a half-German baby or, even worse, if the father's name and details had been revealed, the authorities may have traced him, and he and Christine would have married.

I suddenly realised that if I had gone through the official channels to trace my mother I would have been given access to this form and would have believed all that was said about my father. I feel certain that Christine would have been happier to let me believe that. Anyway, I would never have known about my real father.

This gave me the incentive to look for him.

14

Finding Werner

The search for my father was going to be much harder than finding my mother. Looking for someone in a foreign country, with no Internet access available at that time, I sensed this could take a while. I even doubted the details Christine had given me. Not that she had lied, but forty-four years had passed since she had last spoken his name. I felt it best not to tell her I would be looking for Werner; I did not want to upset her, or for her to ask me not to.

She had told me she had heard of a coach crash in Scotland where German POWs had been killed, so my first task was to check he had not died in England or Scotland. No, he had not. I then started to contact any organisation with German links. My godmother, Win, was a volunteer at the Public Records Office in Kew and she sent me information on POW camps in England – which sadly was of no help as they did not hold lists of names.

I badly needed help to contact the necessary organisations in Germany. It was at this time I was at a party and was introduced to a lovely German lady called Heidi Huber. As we chatted, I mentioned my father was German and I was trying to trace him. Heidi instantly offered to translate letters for me. In fact, as time went on she became much more than a translator and was a great support.

My first letter was to the International Committee of the Red Cross in Geneva. They hold the records of POWs. They quickly responded but warned me that the enquiries could take several months, even a year, as they were very busy assisting the current victims of conflict.

Letters flew from England to Germany – the organisation in Germany which held military records, the British Embassy and the British Consulate-General in every large city in Germany. Every friend and contact I had in Germany was asked to look for Werner Braukmann. Heidi even had relations looking through telephone books. We had decided to concentrate on the Ruhr area, as Christine had told me Werner's mother had died in the bombing in about 1943 in what was to become West Germany.

I wrote to every W. Braukmann we found and received some wonderful letters in reply. Only one suggested what I was doing was a little risky. Most were very helpful; some even said they had been POWs and wished I could have been their daughter.

This was a typical letter

March 1st, 1994
Dear Mrs Coates,
I am sorry, but I can't help you directly. My father's name was Wilhelm and he never was a prisoner of war in Great Britain, though I would be happy to have a younger sister. My uncle's name was Heinz, he wasn't a soldier during the war, and both died years ago. But I would like to help you. First is important, that the correct name is Braukmann, because more people's name is Brauckmann, the pronunciation is the same. I send you a list of Braukmanns in Essen

and Dortmund, both towns are in the Ruhr-district and were bombed in 1943 and 1944 very strong. Maybe, you are successful with these addresses. If not, I will help you to find more in other towns. Most Braukmanns are living in the Ruhr-area, but I know, that there are some more in other regions of the western part of Germany.

My English is not too good, I am sorry. But if you will, you can write me, whenever you need help.

Good luck!

H.D. Braukmann

As I began to tell friends and family about my father, people's reactions were very mixed. Jonathan's witty response was, 'Oh no! My grandfather was a war hero . . . on the other side.' Most people of my age or younger were just interested, but for a few older people, it brought back bitter memories of the war years.

Many people asked me if I felt German. I could certainly see that some of my traits were rather German; my love of order, for instance. I also found something rather disturbing happened at this time – I had to appear amused at all the goose-stepping and 'Heil Hitler' actions people seemed to think so very funny. Suddenly the amount of racism (for that is all you could call it) I saw on television programmes and read in the newspapers became more obvious. I realised that Germans living in Britain had to put up with this nearly daily.

I felt the best way ahead was to learn more about Germany and particularly about the Second World War. Fortunately plenty of books were available at the library. After a few months, I felt I had learned a few obvious truths.

1. Power can be a dangerous thing when mixed with madness and most dictators seem to have had the same DNA.

2. There are good and evil people in every nationality. The good will rise above the situation and make amazing sacrifices for others, and the evil will have the opportunity to abuse, torture and kill with no conscience.
3. When the enemy or an ethnic group are looked upon as sub-human, they are treated as such.

Sadly, we seem not to have learnt from history.

A year of detective work went by. I carried on with normal life but would often think of my father and wonder how he was. Sometimes I would see a coach-load of German tourists and wonder if he was one of the elderly men.

That Easter, Gerald and I, with our son Paul, were at Spring Harvest. We were sitting in our chalet when I found myself saying, 'I think I'll stop looking for my father. It's been a year since I started. I've spent a lot of time and money on the search. Maybe he emigrated after the war. Perhaps he's even dead.'

Gerald and Paul just nodded; it was my decision.

But then, in the silence, I felt God speak to me.

'Don't worry, you will hear from him soon.'

It was so clear that when I returned home two days later I looked through the pile of mail, expecting to find a letter from him. The next day I rushed down the stairs when I heard the postman. No letter from Germany.

However, it came as no surprise to me when, on the next day, Wednesday 6 April 1994 the letter had arrived. Yes, a letter from my father. I later worked out he was probably writing it at the time I had the experience of God speaking so directly!

Of course, it was in German and I had already received letters from Werner Braukmanns. But I knew this was the one as I recognised 'German Red Cross',

'Jones Woodford'. The only strange thing was the spelling of his name – it was *Brauckmann* as so many people had suggested, including the lovely man who had sent me the letter above.

I quickly phoned Heidi with the news and she invited me to take the letter to her home straight away. Feeling very emotional, I drove to Weybridge. Heidi, her husband Hugo and I sat down with tears in our eyes, and they translated the first words I had ever heard from my own father.

April 1st, 1994
Dear Mrs Anona Coates,
Through the German Red Cross I have learnt that you are looking for me, and thus is how I got your address. I have been separated from your natural mother because of the troubles of war. I have been in a further five different camps, and thus lost all addresses and items of value. From Germany I have written to your grandparents 'Family Jones, Woodford Cheshire', but I received no reply.

I am sixty-nine years old, married and retired but my health leaves things to be desired.

I am happy that you have got in touch. I hope that we shall get acquainted a bit through letters and that we shall then meet personally. I would be very happy to get some mail from you. Please, write how you have fared, and why you have heard only now that you have a German father. Also, how is your natural mother? It would be nice if you could write in German, but on the other hand it would be no problem as my wife's son can speak English.

My English got forgotten. As I have had two strokes, I cannot write any more, my wife is doing this for me.

Looking forward to your letter,
Werner Brauckmann

I was so moved; completely thrilled. He was *glad* I had found him and he wanted to get to know me! I instantly wrote a letter telling the story of finding out I was adopted, making contact with Christine and eventually hearing about him. I included a little about myself, Gerald, and my sons. Heidi typed it in German there and then and I gathered lots of photos and posted it as soon as possible.

The next letter from Werner told me more of his story. He just could not comprehend how he had become a father and grandfather in a fortnight! He also enclosed some photographs, including some of himself while in the Luftwaffe and as a POW.

After the war he trained as a locksmith and became a Master Mechanic and Locksmith. He married his first wife, Helga, in 1950 but she died at the age of fifty-five. They had no children. Two years later, he married his second wife, also Helga (it saved changing everything, he joked). Helga had two grown-up children from an earlier marriage.

Strangely, he had wanted to be an interior designer or window dresser but his father had said it was 'breadless art'. He loved to draw and enjoyed oil painting. Since retiring nine years before, his hobby had been gardening. The photos showed a very pleasant German-looking house in the country not far from Dortmund.

Werner's mother Katarina had died in the bombing in April 1943, and his father Richard remarried, dying many years later. His two brothers, Walter and Erich, were drafted and sent out to the Eastern Front, both returning safely after the war. It struck me that it was rather poignant that the three sons had gone to war and survived but their mother had been bombed in her own home and had died in hospital the next day. She was only forty-nine, and Erich had returned from Russia on leave at the time.

Werner and Helga wanted to know more about our church and Gerald's work; I think they thought we belonged to some strange sect. Werner was a Catholic but said it was 'more in his heart' as he did not attend church regularly.

He seemed so happy I had found him. But, thinking I had grown up with Christine's family, he could not understand why it had taken me so long to get in contact. He spoke very warmly of Christine and obviously felt bad that he had not been able to be there for her. When he'd heard nothing from the Jones family he felt he was not needed and had started to rebuild his life in Germany.

With Heidi's help, our letters went to and fro and it was fascinating to hear more about his experiences during the war. He'd been called up in 1941 at the age of seventeen. He said he'd had no desire to fight so decided to do as much training as possible and volunteered for the Luftwaffe. His training took a year in various bases in Germany, Poland and Czechoslovakia.

In 1943, he flew the first of forty-eight missions from a base in Sicily to North Africa, mainly carrying cargo with two fighter planes to protect him. When the war started to go badly for Germany in Africa, he was transferred to Poland where he trained for the Parachute Regiment. Apparently the men had to practice their jumps from high buildings as there was a shortage of planes. In 1944, he was sent to France and later to Holland.

It was from Holland he flew two missions to England on bombing raids. On the second his target was an air base near Oxford. The three planes followed the River Thames towards Oxford; there was a blackout of course. As they neared their target they came under attack from American anti-aircraft fire, and all three planes were hit.

Werner was the only survivor. He managed to bail out and parachute down. Taken prisoner, he was unconscious for a week in an American field hospital. His recovery took eleven weeks.

At that time, it was decided to move some of the German prisoners from Britain in case of a German invasion. Those captured by the British went to Canada and those taken prisoner by the Americans were sent to America. Werner was one of those. In the December of that year he was put on a ship in Liverpool bound for New York. The journey took sixteen days.

The prisoners moved across America staying in camps in thirteen different states until, in 1946, they left Los Angeles for the three-week trip to Comrie in Wales. The next move was to various camps in the south of England and then to Woodford where my father stayed for eighteen months and knew Christine for about nine of those months.

After Christine was sent away (but not because of that), he was sent to Perth in Scotland where he worked on a big estate and tended the garden of an earl. I think this was the happiest period of his imprisonment as the war was well behind him and, for the first time, the prisoners were well fed, especially during the hunting season; he said the English cook looked after them.

His return to Germany started with a move to a camp near Sheffield, then a ship from Harwich to Holland, eventually being released from a camp in Munsterland on 23 March 1948.

The war had taken nearly seven years of Werner's life. Although weakened health-wise by his experiences – he still had a piece of metal in his head from being shot down – at least he was alive and able to return home to a very different Germany and rebuild his life.

I do not recount his experiences in an attempt to make him a hero; he was just one of the millions of young men and women who were swept into a conflict which was not of their choosing and had, somehow, to survive.

Besides, this man was my *father*.

15

Beautiful Daughter

Communication was difficult with my new German family. Heidi was kindly translating our letters but we were planning a visit and I wanted to be able to speak to them in German. Werner said the only English he remembered were phrases he had learnt from the Americans like, 'Take it easy.'

I enrolled at an Adult Education Course to learn 'German for Beginners'. As I had discovered with all the other courses I had been on over the years – pottery, water colouring and interior design – I was the only true beginner! I found out that everyone else was quite fluent already. The German lady who taught us was excellent, giving us a taste of the German culture as well as the language. At the coffee break on the first day, I was asked why I wanted to learn German. I told the story very briefly and the others in the class were fascinated and thrilled I had found my father.

As a person who had not even completed my English education, at forty-five, I found learning a new language very difficult, especially as I did not have the opportunity to use it in everyday life. Still, I did learn how to introduce myself, ask how people were, count, talk about the weather and most importantly order a cup of tea or coffee and even *'eine biere, bitte'*.

Werner and Helga had invited Gerald and me to visit them. As Heidi was visiting friends in Cologne at the same time, she said she would travel to Düsseldorf airport to collect us and drive us to Werner's home. She would stay that day, interpreting for us. My German was certainly not good enough to sustain long conversations! We were to stay in a small hotel nearby and Helga's son Peter would arrive the next day to take over the interpretation.

On 22 July 1994 we flew to visit my father. Although I had already gone through similar emotions when travelling to meet Christine, I felt very strange; quite apprehensive and tearful. As we landed in my Fatherland, I felt I ought to kneel down and kiss the tarmac . . . Fortunately, I didn't. My lips would probably have stuck, as we had landed in the middle of a heatwave.

I had already been to Germany but it felt like the first time. I saw everything with new eyes. Leaving the airport and driving into the country, I was amazed by its beauty.

Heidi was as nervous as we were as we drew up to the house. Werner and Helga greeted us at the door and, as we kissed each other, we were all crying. After a tour of their home – immaculate as I'd expected – and their beautiful garden, we sat down for a cup of strong coffee and began to talk.

With Heidi's help we began to get to know one another, asking all the questions about our lives we could, trying to catch up on so many lost years. I found I really liked Werner; he had a wicked sense of humour and he and Helga laughed a lot. He said he had been very lonely after his first wife died, and had met Helga Number Two in a park, where they'd sat together and started chatting. There was even a photo of Helga Number One on the mantelpiece.

Werner was a better painter than I; several really good oil paintings hung on the walls. He was not at all well, having suffered two strokes and, although he was still driving his Mercedes (I never thought I would have a father with a Mercedes!), he had trouble walking and his hearing was bad.

We were all in tears several times that day. At one point, Werner asked me if I had been happy with my adoptive parents.

I paused for a second and said, 'Yes.'

Heidi's eyes filled up as she translated. Later she said she was amazed that I had told an outright lie. But, in that split second, I'd thought, 'What possible good would it do to tell him the true situation? He was helpless to change the situation when I was a child, and to tell him the truth now will do only harm.' After all, he was an elderly man with many regrets. Many may disagree, but I do feel there is such a thing as a pardonable lie. I think sometimes love truly does cover a multitude of sins.

At lunchtime, we were taken to a beer garden and sat in the shade eating, chatting and taking photos. Then Werner suddenly took my hand. He looked me in the eyes and said, 'I have a beautiful daughter.'

I was so touched, my heart felt full of love and acceptance. After all the years of being told I was ugly by the man I thought was my father, at last I had a father who could say what every daughter needs to hear – that she is beautiful.

After an incredible day, Helga and Werner drove us to the hotel. I slept well that night. After a simple continental breakfast we wandered into the town and bought some flowers at the market. I was very pleased when the woman on the flower stall seemed to understand my German.

Werner and Helga collected us and Peter, who would be with us for the next two days, arrived. Peter had a very open, pleasant personality and spoke excellent English. He got on very well with Gerald. I had not realised that Werner's brother Erich lived only a few doors away, so Erich and his wife Elsbeth came to join us for the day, and we were later taken on a tour of their home which had been tastefully extended. Their son Jürgen, his wife Monika and their three daughters lived with them, but they were away on holiday.

As we sat around the table drinking coffee, with several fans keeping us cool, I was keen to find out how Werner felt about the war years. I knew the facts but not the feelings. It was amazing to hear him talking about that era; I think, for the first time. The whole family sat open-mouthed. He said he had had no political interest but, like his brothers, he'd had no choice in the matter when called up as a teenager. I think he quite enjoyed the training and the camaraderie in the early years.

'Were you terrified when your plane was hit?' I asked.

'No,' he replied, 'there was no time. It was a matter of survival. You had to do what you had been trained to do, to get out.'

He was never ill-treated when a prisoner but being confined was obviously hard. As you can imagine, when they had nothing to do except smoke and kick a ball around, the men became very bored. They were pleased when in America the government said they could work picking cotton or fruit, cutting down trees – anything to pass the time.

'Will I find any American brothers or sisters?' I queried.

'No,' he sadly replied. 'No fraternisation.'

It seemed that the prisoners' main pre-occupation was with food. They were always hungry and were given the last of what was available.

Werner did say that he still had nightmares about the war years – strangely, not about anything that actually happened. He dreamt that he was underground in a kind of dugout, the enemy were advancing, and he could see them. As the other men escaped he tried to gather his things but was too slow; when he tried to run, his legs would not work. He would wake up terrified.

We discussed Werner and Helga coming to visit us but they were unsure. Werner had not been able to fly since that last flight when he had been shot out of the sky.

As our long weekend ended, I felt very satisfied. It had been so good to have Gerald with me and we both felt very much at home. The whole family seemed pleased to have met us and we all looked forward to continuing our new-found relationships.

A week or so later, Christine came to stay for a few days. Now I had met Werner I felt the time was right to tell her about him. We sat out on the patio one evening and, after Gerald had plied her with some white wine, I braced myself.

'After you told me about my father,' I said, 'I thought I'd try to find him.' I took a deep breath. 'Well, I did, and Gerald and I have just been to meet him in Germany.'

'I don't want to know!' She covered her ears. 'I don't want to know. Don't tell me. I don't want to hear about that man.'

I was stunned; to me, her reaction was astounding. She seemed to revert to being a seventeen-year-old, coping with the rejection of her parents, having an illegitimate baby and the father not being there.

'That's OK, that's fine,' I said, quietly. 'I just wanted you to know.'

After a while she calmed down and ventured to ask a few questions.

'What was he like? Do you have any photos?'

Werner had given me a photograph of him, Ernst and another friend taken during the time that Christine knew him. She took it and looked at it.

'I think I took that photo,' she said.

I passed on his greetings and said that he spoke very warmly of her, but more than that she did not want to know.

Then, Werner and Helga wrote one day to say that yes, they would like to make the journey to England to meet all the family. I was thrilled. But it meant a lot of work, trying to find a time when Gerald would be at home, the boys would be free and, even more importantly, when I could arrange for a German-speaking friend to be available. Several people offered but it was very complicated. Eventually, I gave Werner and Helga dates, and also some other dates when I could perhaps visit them, with one of the boys.

I received a letter saying they had booked tickets, not for the dates I had given for them to visit us, but for one of the dates I could visit them! Heidi was away so Marie, her daughter, phoned them to say that it would not be convenient. After that, I received a very sharp letter. They were obviously disappointed, after plucking up the courage to book. They would also lose money on the tickets.

I panicked. 'It's happening again!' I believed I could lose another relationship with a father over a muddle with dates! So I wrote explaining the situation and sent money to cover the amount they had lost. I received a rather curt reply from Helga, telling me I should be more thoughtful and work out my diary properly.

I was determined that this would not sour our relationship and did visit them again. Gerald and I were with church leaders Rudi and Billa Pinke in Frankfurt; Gerald was speaking at their church, Christliches Zentrum. A lovely lady called Connie, who was a member of the congregation, offered to travel with me by train from Frankfurt to see Werner and Helga. We spent a very special day together, but I noticed that Werner's health was worsening. It was quite an effort for him to move around and he was no longer driving.

I began to fear that I would not see him again.

16

Secrets and a Special Moment

Christine looked on me as more of a sister or friend than a daughter, which was understandable as she had not been able to mother me. I was quite happy with that as now, in my forties, I did not need a mother; in fact, I felt more like a mother to Mum, Christine and Werner. I wanted them to be as content as possible in their later years and was determined to protect them from the whole truth. I had not told any of them how Dad had abused me sexually.

As we drove around the countryside near Christine's home, she told me two very strange stories. I began to see that there was a family history of giving away children.

Apparently her mother, Doris, my Gran Jones, had not known who her parents were. She had been fostered by a family in Woodford called Shattwell. Every few months 'a lady' would come to visit, bringing money and new clothes, and would spend time playing with her. One day a letter arrived. Christine told me she'd seen it and it said

Dear Mr and Mrs Shattwell,
Thank you so much for looking after my darling baby daughter. I will be coming to collect her on Saturday.

Christine thought that the surname was Slater and that the letter had come from Rose Hill in Buxton. But the lady never arrived. The Shatwells continued to care for little Doris and brought her up as their own child. It was much later that she discovered the truth. With no birth certificate, it proved difficult to get a passport when, in 1995, she wanted to visit her daughter Kath and family in Seattle. When filling in the forms she put her date of birth and, for her name 'Known as Doris Ellen Shattwell'. I wondered what happened when she was married.

Christine asked me to do some research at St Catherine's House to find out if her mother's birth had been registered but I could find no one of any variation of her name; there was a possibility of her name being Laura Ellen Slater, born around the date given and in the same area. But in all this, I found it very hard to understand how, with such a strange background, Gran Jones had not been able to identify more with me and my need to find my birth family.

Her mother was always referred to as 'a lady' but this did not necessarily mean she was Lady So-and-So; country folk may have felt that anyone dressed in smart town clothes was ladylike. I would love to have seen the letter Christine mentioned; it would have answered so many questions. Perhaps she was a lady who had an affair and needed to hide the child away in the country until her husband died, or they divorced. But what prevented her from collecting the baby? Perhaps he found out! My mind wandered on. Doris was born in April 1908 . . . perhaps her mother was a maid in a big house and King Edward VII, on one of his visits, had bedded her – I always knew I had royal blood! More likely, she was a shop girl and the father an errand boy. The mystery remains.

On another day, Christine obviously wanted to unburden herself and told me this second story.

When she had been sent in disgrace to her uncle and aunt's, it was very difficult for her. The other children in the family and neighbourhood teased her as her pregnancy began to show. The only one who was particularly kind to her was a cousin around her age, Michael. She never forgot this and when, years later after her marriage and the births of Kathryn and Nicholas, she met him again, they fell in love. Dennis and Christine had been going through a difficult time and Michael, who had never married, seemed like an escape. She told me their relationship was not sexual but very intense. They planned to go away together.

'What about the children?' I asked, shocked.

'Oh, Dennis would look after them,' she said, 'and my mother could help.'

Apparently her mother already did a lot of looking after the children, but this time she said no. The reason was even more shocking.

'You *cannot* go away with Michael,' Gran Jones had told her, 'he could be your half-brother!' Apparently, she'd explained, 'I had an affair with his father, Bert, and he may have been *your* father.' Bert was, of course, her brother-in-law.

Understandably, that was the end of Christine and Michael's relationship, although they stayed in touch. But Christine said she did not really believe her mother and thought she'd told her the story just to stop her leaving with Michael. I doubt that. For someone as upright as Gran Jones to tell her own daughter something that put her in a bad light would have been impossible. Only the fact that they could have been brother and sister would have forced her to confess.

I found it hard to understand how Christine could have ever considered leaving her two children; perhaps having already given up one child made it easier. The Christine I knew loved her grown-up children and adored her grandchildren but I suppose passions run high when we're young.

During August 1996, Gerald and I booked two weeks' holiday in our diaries. A journalist called Steve Selthoeffer had invited Gerald to speak at some large events to be put on for the troops in Sarajevo. The Christian band Delirious? was to be the main attraction. Plans were moving forward and we were being briefed as to how to behave in a war zone. Then, the military cancelled the trip. The Bosnian elections were coming up; it would be a very volatile time and the troops did not need civilians getting in the way.

We decided to stay at home and perhaps travel up to London or drive down to the coast. I put it to Gerald that I had always wanted to see my birthplace and he kindly agreed to make a trip to Wellington in Shropshire.

After a pleasant night in the Holiday Inn in Telford, we drove to Wellington. I had already phoned ahead for directions and we soon found the Priory Nursing Home. It was now a residential home for the elderly but you could still see that before becoming the private nursing home I was born in, it had started life as a rather nice Georgian house. I took a few photos and tried to imagine what it had been like that dark evening in 1947 when a frightened young girl had been taken in to give birth.

Leaving Wellington we followed on the map the route to Waters Upton, the village where Christine had lived with Uncle Bert, Aunty Gladys and their children. Waters Upton was a tiny village and we soon found Sytch Lane. The row of houses was on one side of the road with fields dropping away on the other.

I don't know that I have ever been in such a quiet place. It was about one o'clock on a hot August day; nothing stirred, and no one was about. We had no idea which house was the right one and there was nobody to ask. Suddenly, an elderly lady appeared and began to water her front garden – rather unusual at that time of day in the heat of the sun.

'I'm sure that lady has lived here all her life,' I said. 'She'll know which house it is.' I jumped out of the car and asked her if she remembered the Jones family.

'Yes,' she said, immediately, 'Gladys and Bert.'

Then she mentioned Vera, the aunt who, with Aunty Gladys, had taken me to London. She even remembered Christine staying.

'I held you as a baby!' she beamed.

We were busy chatting with the lady – she was called Mrs Ralph – about the family, when she asked, 'Would you like to go into the house?' It turned out that her nephew had just bought it and was modernising it as we spoke! He seemed quite happy for us to wander around. Other than a new fitted kitchen, it was very like the council house I'd lived in as a baby – complete with outside privy.

We took more photographs and left Waters Upton amazed that we had probably met the only person in the village who had known me as a baby!

And I knew that this was a special moment that God had given me.

17

Saying Goodbye

Negotiations had begun in August 1998 with a view to Gerald and me moving to oversee the running of Waverley Abbey House near Farnham in Surrey. CWR (Crusade for World Revival), the Christian publishing and counselling organisation, had bought the house several years before in a derelict state. After much hard work and restoration it was opened in 1987 as a Training and Conference Centre.

Selwyn Hughes, the founder of CWR, the CWR board and John Muys, the CEO, held many meetings with us. Eventually it was decided that we would form a new board called KLM (Kingdom Life Ministries) to run the house. A new manager was appointed and I was asked to oversee presentation, marketing and run the front of house office.

In the New Year, we officially took over the running of the house so travelled down during the week, sometimes staying overnight. Our house in Esher was under offer and we were remodelling three bedrooms on the top floor of Waverley Abbey House to make an apartment that we would rent. We felt the venture would not work unless we lived on the premises.

Gerald's staff at the Pioneer office moved from Walton-on-Thames and started renting space at

Waverley Abbey House for Gerald, the Pioneer Trust and March for Jesus. CWR, who owned the house, would obviously retain their offices and continue to hold their training events and counselling courses as usual. CWR and Pioneer would work alongside one another – with very diverse ministries, they were able to form an alliance.

As soon as our apartment was ready, we moved down. As we were downsizing our own living space we had pictures, ornaments and plants spare. When I was a child I dreamt of owning a doll's house and, as Gerald and I walked around the beautiful Georgian mansion hanging pictures and reorganising the rooms, I felt that I had been given a giant-size one.

Many of the skills I had learnt over the years came in very useful during this time. I really enjoyed upgrading the guest bedrooms with new bed linen and towels, tea and coffee facilities and chocolates on the pillows. When some of the rooms needed redecorating I was very happy to help with choosing the new décor.

Building up the business of the conference centre was very rewarding and it was wonderful to live in such a beautiful setting overlooking a lake, the ruins of Waverley Abbey, the River Wey and the woodland beyond. We even heard the sound of battle as the Romans and Germanians fought each other during the filming of *Gladiator* in the Forestry Commission woodland further on. On quieter evenings, to sit on the balcony with a drink after everyone had gone home and watch the wild black rabbits play and the deer looking on, was idyllic.

Living 'above the shop' did have its downside, though. We had very little privacy and no door to separate us off from the public part of the building. I always felt on duty even if I was not and, being the only people living in the house, I felt responsible for the security – especially if Gerald was away, as that meant I was on my own overnight in a sixteen-bedroom house.

We were not lonely, though; we were part of the community of staff who came in every day and the guests, some very regular, who we got to know well. Some of the friendships formed at that time have continued to this day.

Because we had sold our own house and were renting at Waverley, Gerald and I felt we should buy some property ready for when we would need our own home again. He was spending a lot of time in London with church leaders and MPs, so it seemed sensible to look for a home there. We found the perfect flat in Regency Street, Westminster – very small with two bedrooms, just modernised and in a small gated block complete with communal garden and porter. We enjoyed buying the few modern pieces of furniture to equip it, very different from our traditionally furnished apartment in Waverley Abbey House.

Around this time, I noticed that Christine had been getting more forgetful and muddled. She had developed breast cancer and had very bad backache. Eventually, she was diagnosed with Alzheimer's. The last time I spoke to her, it was very sad. By then, she did not always answer the phone, but this time, she did.

'Yes?'

'Hello, it's Anona here.'

'Who?'

Then she dropped the phone.

That was our last conversation.

It was very difficult for Kathryn and Nick as they had to deal with the everyday problems that occurred. The time came when Christine could not stay at home on her own and had to go into a care home. I did not see her there but it must have been traumatic for Kathryn and Nick to see their mother deteriorate in body and mind. I must admit that as I prayed for her, I asked God not to let this continue.

When the phone call came to say that she had died, I felt very upset but relieved she was no longer in pain and confusion. How grateful I was that I had found her and that we had several good years getting to know one another.

Kathryn and Nick kindly asked me to speak at her funeral. Gerald and I, with our three sons, drove up to Manchester. As we walked into the packed church for the service, people gasped. Some had never seen me before and they were shocked to see a woman so much like Christine.

When I publicly shared how I had found Christine and how we had been welcomed into the family, many were in tears.

As I looked at the coffin I said, 'Christine's body and mind have let her down but her spirit is now free and she is whole and happy with God.'

I believe that to be true.

18

Compassion

As charismatic Christians, we believe that God will speak to us and direct us through words of prophecy. A few years before, when we were living in Esher, an American, Dale Gentry, was visiting our church. He was a dynamic preacher and had the gift of prophecy which, over the years, we had seen was accurate. Gerald and I had received prophecies from God many times – prophecies which had helped us make the right decisions and had encouraged us. (Gerald himself has this gift and God has used it to bless many.)

In a meeting of several hundred people held at Downsend School in Leatherhead, Dale suddenly picked me out and said, 'Anona, you will be the source of supply for thousands of children.'

I burst into tears; this was my heart's desire. I had never forgotten the daydream I had as a child when I would gather children into a home, love them and provide for them.

Gerald and I had sponsored several children and students over the years and had been guardians for others but . . . *thousands* of children! How could that be? I knew that with prophecies you cannot force anything to occur, but I did begin to get very frustrated when, a year or so later, I seemed no nearer to seeing anything happen. Several people contacted me about their favourite charities but I did not feel I should get involved with them.

Then, one day, the phone in our lounge at Waverley rang. It was Tony Neeves, an old friend I had not heard from for a while. Tony had been working for Tear Fund, one of the biggest Christian charities in the UK. Their work was mainly overseas in Third World countries with disaster relief, development and sponsorship. In fact, when our boys were growing up we sponsored a boy in Burma called Naw Awng and later a student in Nigeria, both through Tear Fund. I had noticed, when their letters arrived (a very important part of sponsorship), that they were headed 'Compassion'. This was the name of the charity based in America which Tear Fund had been administrating in the UK. An office was to open in October 1999 for Compassion UK. A board of trustees was being put together and Tony asked if I would consider being one.

I did not need much time to think about it. Gerald and I both felt that this was the right thing to do and the fulfilment of the prophecy. There was no way I could personally supply the needs of thousands of children but the decisions I, as a board member, would make, would literally affect thousands. In fact, since we began, well over forty-five thousand children have now been sponsored by wonderful caring people in the UK.

Being involved with Compassion has proved to be one of the most fulfilling things I have done. As a board member, I was given the opportunity to visit Haiti, one of the twenty-three countries the children live in. Haiti, with a population of 7.5 million, is in the Caribbean, not far from Cuba, and is part of an island it shares with the Dominican Republic.

Years of corrupt government, and the belief that AIDS entered the USA through the cruise ships which stopped there, has meant that there is no tourism and no aid coming from wealthy countries. The few rich families send their children abroad to be educated. The churches have schools attached to them and Compassion works with the Protestant churches but the main religion in Haiti is Catholic/Voodoo.

Our team, led by Tony and Ian Hamilton, the Compassion UK CEO, left Heathrow for New York. As we waited there for our plane to Port-Au-Prince I chatted to a man in the queue. He asked where I was going.

'Haiti,' I replied.

'Why?' he asked, in a shocked voice. Apparently only missionaries and aid workers venture there.

This visit gave me the chance to see how Compassion works, starting with the sponsor making the decision to take on the commitment of a child – sometimes more than one – through the office in Weybridge, Surrey, where everything is administered, to the child receiving the benefits of all that love and care.

Haiti should be a beautiful place, but years of neglect and poverty have wrecked it. The people are amazingly resilient, but there is an underlying feeling of fear. Our team settled in one of the few very nice hotels in the hills surrounding Port-Au-Prince. The view from the veranda was amazing; from that distance we could not tell that the built-up areas we saw were actually slums. In the two weeks we spent there I only saw a few roads and buildings that had been finished and they were in the wealthy areas. Many people lived with sewage on one side and rubbish on the other; no wonder so many gangs of men in the slums accepted money to fight for the government, or for the opposition. As usual, the sick, the children and elderly were the ones to suffer the most and that is where Compassion came in.

After meeting the dedicated staff at the Compassion office, we were taken out to visit the first of many projects. The children were smart in their uniforms; they obviously loved school. Although the equipment was very basic, they were receiving a good education. A healthy meal was served at lunchtime, the only meal many would receive that day. The headmaster introduced us to several teachers. These young men had been Compassion children and were now giving back to their community. I think this was what I found the most moving; Compassion had been in Haiti for over thirty years and these educated young people could get a job in America or Canada but had chosen to stay. Compassion's motto is 'One life at a time' but that one life can affect so many and change a nation.

Compassion UK and the partners from other countries between them provide for nearly a million children worldwide. Sixty thousand in Haiti alone. The projects were schools attached to churches, some small, some very large. Not all the children were sponsored; some parents had jobs and could pay towards the child's education, others paid for uniforms or books. I asked how the children were chosen and learnt they were carefully assessed and children were taken from different families to spread the benefits amongst the community. Brought up in that environment, most of the children became Christians, some becoming pastors or church workers.

At each project we visited, we were taken to the houses of a couple of the children. These were very basic concrete buildings, usually one room, sometimes with a bed and very occasionally a table and chairs. Clothes hung on a string in the corner, cooking was done outside and I saw no toilets. In the country the families often had a pig or a goat and chickens. Everyone had to walk quite a way to get water in massive plastic containers; usually the women carried them on their heads.

One of the very sad situations we encountered was the plight of the children sent from the countryside to relations in the city with the hope of a better life. Often the children are no more than slaves, beaten, sexually abused and forced to work. Compassion had arranged for these *restavek* (stay with) children to go to school part-time. I will never forget the dead expression in their eyes and I pray that by now they will know they are loved and will have hope in their lives for a better future.

Near the end of our trip, we were taken by boat to the island of La Gonave. I was sure that the boat we were on was the same one Christopher Columbus had arrived in when he first discovered Haiti, but it was good to feel the sea air.

The journey over the mountains to the projects was not so good, but as the only female on that part of the trip, I was allowed to sit in the cab of the truck with the driver while the guys all bumped along in the back. It was worth it, though; we visited two schools and, even though it was a Saturday, they had all turned out to receive us and had even put on a barbeque on the beach.

On the return journey (during which our truck had two punctures), we saw three children with their donkey slowly climbing the mountain road. Further along, their mother was waiting by the roadside for them. It had taken them about one and a half hours to get that far and this was the journey they made every day to get to school and back.

On La Gonave, we stayed at the Wesleyan Mission, where we were made very welcome. Part of the Mission housed the hospital, the only one on the island. The dedication of the staff was incredible – most were Haitian but there was also a Canadian family. The facilities were very basic and, apparently, if anyone was seriously ill they called in a doctor from Cuba.

A few years before, a ferry had sunk between La Gonave and the Haitian mainland. It was overloaded and more than eight hundred people drowned; 100 orphans were taken in by other family members but there was no money for the children's education. The church leaders there appealed to Compassion for help. We discussed the situation and, after our return home, at the next board meeting I put it to the trustees that out of our unrestricted funds we paid for four years education for the children. It was unanimously agreed.

Since my visit, Haiti has been brought to the attention of the western world because of a bloody coup which ousted the president, Jean Bertrand Aristide (and also, because of a terrible flood). UN troops were posted there to keep the peace.

As most people say after coming back from this kind of trip, 'It was truly a life-changing experience for me.' Well, for me, that was really so. I found it very difficult when I returned home; after living amongst such poverty everything seemed so excessive.

I have always felt committed to sponsorship as a way of giving but it was wonderful to see, in the flesh, the difference it makes to a child. Not just the money because, of course, they don't see that; but to understand that someone in another country knows about you, takes time to write and pray and *believes* in you, is very powerful. The two little girls Gerald and I sponsor in India write, 'Dear Mama, I love you.' A very humbling experience . . . but to be involved in helping thousands of children – yes, that was indeed a dream come true.

19

A Home for Anona

Our time at Waverley Abbey House was coming to an end now; Gerald and I were looking for accommodation for the Pioneer office and also a home for us.

In one sense we could have moved anywhere – people were always asking Gerald to be part of what they were doing church-wise, even abroad. We did have our flat in London but it was too small to live in all the time and our main contacts there were now leaving. Our good friends R.T. and Louise Kendall from Westminster Chapel were off to the States and Archbishop George and Eileen Carey were retiring. We seemed drawn back to the area we had moved from, but not particularly Cobham or Esher.

Our church, Pioneer People, had recently taken on the lease of the Thorndike Theatre in Leatherhead. It had been closed for several years and was in a sad state. We had all donned rubber gloves and old clothes to rid it of all the dead pigeons and to restore it to its former glory. Now renamed 'The Theatre', we held church events there, put on films and shows and let it out for conference bookings. Our desire was not just for The Theatre to be open but for us to be part of the revival of Leatherhead itself. It had recently been dubbed 'The

Worst High Street in England', rather unfairly I thought. The closing of the theatre, the pedestrianisation of the high street and parking problems had, however, all contributed to it losing business. Although Leatherhead was not dead, it was certainly feeling very unwell.

Gerald and I had never moved to another church; even living in Farnham, where there was a great Pioneer church, we had still driven up to various other venues (and later, The Theatre) for church meetings and that was where our commitment was. It made sense to live near Leatherhead. We would also be back close to two of our sons – Paul was living in Cobham and Simon in Molesey. Jonathan would buy his own place in London. I would also be nearer Mum; she still lived in Effingham with Vic and his wife Dee sharing the home.

Never in my life have I written a wish list but this time I did. I asked God for a home containing three bedrooms, a study for Gerald, an open fireplace, parking and a garden. I was desperate for my own garden again. At the bottom, in large capitals, I wrote, CHARACTER. All the houses I had already seen were singularly lacking in that quality. I presented my list to God. Now, I know that he doesn't always give us what we want, but I think this time he took pity on me – for, the next property I viewed, in Great Bookham, had all of the above including an inglenook fireplace and old beams. The cottage dated from 1550 and had character oozing from it.

Gerald was busy that day so my friend Robyn, who lived nearby, came with me to view it.

Afterwards, as we stood on the pavement outside, I said, 'I love it.'

I then had the strangest experience. I suddenly remembered that as a child, I had often walked past this cottage and one day I had looked at it, peered in the window and thought, 'What a lovely old house.' It was as if I had come home! This was strange in itself, as the last place I had *ever* wanted to live was near to the house I had grown up in. The whole area held too many unhappy memories. Incredibly, I found I felt the opposite; I began to look forward to returning. God was healing my past.

We moved down from London on my birthday, 3 December 2002. The survey had uncovered lots of work that needed doing. Miraculously, so near to Christmas, I had managed to organise plumbers, electricians, roofers etc. to do much of the work in the two weeks before we moved from Waverley with most of our furniture and possessions. A new kitchen was fitted and once the cleaning and decorating was finished the old house came alive; every visitor, even small children, said they felt safe and welcome in it.

Our new cottage had quite a history. It was built in the sixteenth century as a timber-framed house, and over the next few centuries it was 'modernised'. The walls were bricked in, an inglenook fireplace added and a cellar dug. Sometime before 1780 it became the White Hart Inn. In 1819 the name was changed to the Saracen and Ring Inn. Then in 1895, Mrs Chrystie, a Quaker and ardent temperance worker, bought the Inn and closed it down! It was later resold as a private dwelling and, in the 1960s, divided into two cottages, one of which we bought.

We were thrilled when Simon said as a gift he would like to landscape our front garden. I had always dreamt of a cottage garden with a picket fence and lavender and roses.

It was time for me to look for a job now I didn't work at Waverley any more. I really wanted it to be part-time and local. Seeing an advert for staff at Polesden Lacey, the large National Trust house nearby, I filled in my CV for the first time in my life. Though lacking in qualifications I seemed to have fitted in quite a lot of experiences – shop assistant, window dresser, interior designer, doctor's receptionist, prison volunteer, licensee, assistant manager of conference centre, along with marketing and public speaking etc. But I did not get the job! Perhaps I was overqualified.

Moving to a new area, we had signed on with a new doctor and off I went for a new patient health check.

Running through a list of questions, the doctor asked, 'Are you working at the moment?'

'No, I'm looking for a job locally.' I added with a laugh, 'In fact, I used to be a doctor's receptionist.'

'Give your name in at the desk,' he replied. 'We're looking for a new receptionist.'

I was offered the job and, after a crash course on the computer side of the work, I felt very much at home. I also started at The Theatre, working for the renamed The Leatherhead Revival Trust, one evening a week as duty manager when films or shows were on, and I did a few hours a week as a volunteer, welcoming people and answering the many queries. I was later asked to manage the café at The Theatre, which I did for nine months, four of those while still working at the surgery!

And so, Gerald and I settled very happily into our new home and felt very much a part of the community.

Mum was now beginning to show her age. Fortunately, living with Vic and Dee, she had help and company in the evenings and weekends. I was happy to take her to the doctor, the opticians and to hospital appointments during the week. She loved going to the local garden centre where we would buy food for all her animals, fish weed and new plants, and then have lunch. I noticed that she was gradually walking and eating less. She was

diabetic and suffered badly from arthritis, but her mind
was still very alert.

Just after Christmas 2003, she fell at home and broke
her leg. For the first time in her long life – she was now
in her mid-eighties – she was hospitalised and she hated
it. Over the next ten weeks she deteriorated. Although
her leg had been operated on she was too scared to try
and walk; twice she went into a diabetic coma, and massive gall stones were discovered. After catching a urine
infection, she started to hallucinate. She was very upset
thinking that the nurses were hitting her, and imagining
Dad was in the ward. She then contracted MRSA.

We took turns in visiting her so she had visitors every
day. I would often leave in tears after seeing her so
unhappy and in such pain. Several of my friends had
lost parents recently and were devastated by this; never
having been that close to Mum I had felt sad that I
would not experience much emotion on her death. Yet,
oddly, I felt a real, growing love for her.

Although she had been very happy to come to church
events for retired people, she had never really spoken
about her beliefs or faith. Now, at the end of each visit, I
would pray for her and read from the Gideon's Bible the
Lord's Prayer and the twenty-third psalm. This seemed
to comfort her. I would always kiss her goodbye and
say, 'I love you, Mum, and God loves you.'

One day she mumbled something and then said, 'You
didn't hear that, did you?'

I leant towards her.

'I love you, too,' she repeated.

That was the first time she had ever said that to me.

During this time, Gerald and I travelled to Lowestoft
to attend the Pioneer Leaders' Conference. A friend from
church, Anne Marshall, offered to visit Mum while I was
away. Mum knew Anne from the times she came to

church events and was apparently pleased to see her. One of the things Anne did was to buy Mum a cuddly toy, a lion.

Then, Mum asked Anne to pray for her.

Anne said, 'Of course I will! But you can pray for yourself.' She then very naturally led Mum in a prayer asking for forgiveness and new life in Jesus.

I was thrilled when Anne phoned me to tell me what had happened. Seeing Mum so ill I'd really wanted to ask God to take her but I was not sure of her eternal destination.

Returning from the conference, I talked with Mum to make sure she knew what she had prayed and that she understood it. She did, and on the next few visits seemed to find peace when I talked to her about God's love. I now started to pray earnestly that her life would not be prolonged unnecessarily. It was still a shock, though, when at 3 a.m. one Sunday morning a nurse phoned to say that she had 'passed away'.

Vic asked me to organise Mum's funeral. I felt very honoured. She was to be buried with Dad at St Lawrence's Church in Effingham. Father Charles, the vicar, was wonderful, very sensitive and understanding of the atmosphere I wanted. We chose some suitable music, not at all depressing. Gerald read from Luke chapter 15, the parables that Jesus told of the lost sheep, the lost coin and the lost son, then Father Charles gave a great sermon and I shared how at the end of her very sad and difficult life, Mum had found peace with God and was enjoying his presence.

Mum was buried with her childhood teddy bear and, at her request, the cuddly toy lion Anne had given her. Family and friends came back to the cottage for refreshments; this wasn't a sad time as we were all glad that Mum was free at last.

I felt very privileged that I was able to speak at both my mothers' funerals and I know I will see them again.

20

And Today . . .?

As I finish writing my story, I am amazed; I'm a very ordinary woman, the illegitimate child of a teenager and an enemy prisoner, adopted into a family where I was rejected and abused. But today, I have found healing in many areas of my life, although I am still learning.

Because of my experiences in the past, I can easily be negative and lapse into feelings of rejection. Losses of friends and relationships because of death, disagreements or moves affect me badly; I take it very personally. Lies and unfair judgements about Gerald or people I know upset me greatly, but God always seems to give me the grace to forgive and I find it very hard to hold a grudge.

If I have any regrets, it is my lack of education but I seem to have managed without one. And what am I most proud of? My three sons! They are a book in themselves. They are each their own man, as we had hoped; very different in character, personality and gifting. Paul is now Director of Centres for the YMCA, combining his gift of compassion with his skill in administration. He met a lovely lady called Lisa, who he knew in his teens. They were married by Gerald in our garden in August 2007 and we are now proud grandparents to Lola, Lisa's daughter from a previous marriage. Simon is a very hard worker and uses his creative skills in his landscape gardening. Always the life and soul of the party, someone once said to me, 'Is he the one who is always smiling?' Jonathan works in an investment bank in the City of London. He and Joanna, his fiancée, are looking forward to their wedding and future life together.

As for church, we are at a very exciting stage of the journey. We meet at The Theatre on a Sunday morning and are blessed to have many gifted and committed young people as part of our congregation. Some have even moved into the area to be involved in what is happening. Leatherhead has blossomed over the last few years, with many new shops and restaurants opening. Town's people have told us that The Theatre re-opening and Christians in the area working together for the benefit of the community have contributed to a more pleasant place to live and work in.

As Gerald's sixtieth birthday approached, several of his good friends suggested we arrange something special for him. A surprise party was held at The Theatre and nearly five hundred people attended the 'This is Your Life' celebration. Steve Chalke, the church leader and broadcaster, hosted the afternoon and amid the fun, music and surprises one thing stood out. *Everyone* expressed how Gerald had encouraged them in their Christian life. One of the first was the painfully shy fifteen-year-old girl he made welcome on her first day at work.

People often ask me if I am glad I found out the truth about my origins and discovered my natural family. Although at times it has been very emotional, I do not regret a moment. I have not seen my remaining parent, Werner, for a few years but we keep in touch by letter. Nick and Jacqui, with their teenage children, Sam and

Kirsten, emigrated to New Zealand to start an exciting new life. Kathryn, wonderfully, found faith in God and this has sustained her through some very difficult years. She is now very happy with her lovely new husband, Dave. Her daughters, Charlotte and Rebecca, who were tiny when I first met them, are now young women pursuing their dreams.

We had a sad loss in 2007 when Gerald's brother Roy died, aged only fifty-nine. He is greatly missed by all his family.

Vic and Dee live nearby in the house Vic and I grew up in; that was to be expected, for Dad had always said Vic would 'get the house'. Vic and his wife have worked hard and transformed the house and garden into a light and attractive home, nothing like the dark and fear-filled place I remember.

When I look back now and think of that little girl who so wistfully said, 'I wish I was,' when her friend told her she was adopted, I can see how God has blessed me. More than I could ever have imagined.

Postscript

Around twenty years ago, I was with Gerald at a church in Los Angeles. I was speaking at a women's meeting, sharing the story of my childhood, and how I had become a Christian – this was before I found out about my secret past. I told the women how God had given me strength to forgive my family. People were in tears, and I was able to pray with them. Then, the pastor and his wife had a prophecy for me: God had told them I would one day write a book about my story. And they gave me a token of the prophecy – a pen.

I forgot about this, although I used the pen practically every day (with new cartridges of course!).

It was only when this book was accepted by Authentic that I realised I was signing the contract – with the pen that was given to me all those years ago.

Useful Contacts

If you have been affected by issues raised in this book and would like to contact Anona, you can write to her at:

Anona Coates
c/o Authentic Media
9 Holdom Avenue
Bletchley
Milton Keynes
MK1 1QR
England

Care for the Family
www.care-for-the-family.org.uk

ChildLine
Tel: 0800 1111
www.childline.org.uk

Compassion UK
www.compassionuk.org

Lifecentre: SUST
Support for Unwanted Sexual Trauma
Tel: 01243 779196
www.lifecentre.uk.com

NORCAP Supporting Adults Affected by Adoption
www.norcap.org.uk

Pioneer
www.pioneer.org.uk

AMANDA LORD WITH SIMON LORD

SEARCH FOR A FATHER

**THE AMAZING TRUE STORY OF
ONE WOMAN'S SEARCH FOR HER FATHER**

FOREWORD BY
MARTIN SMITH [DELIRIOUS?]
& DARLENE ZSCHECH [HILLSONG]

978-1-86024-575-6

Jeff Lucas

Helen Sloane's Diary

978-1-85078-797-6

NICK BATTLE

Big
Boys
Don't
Cry

The autobiography
of Nick Battle

978-1-86024-612-8

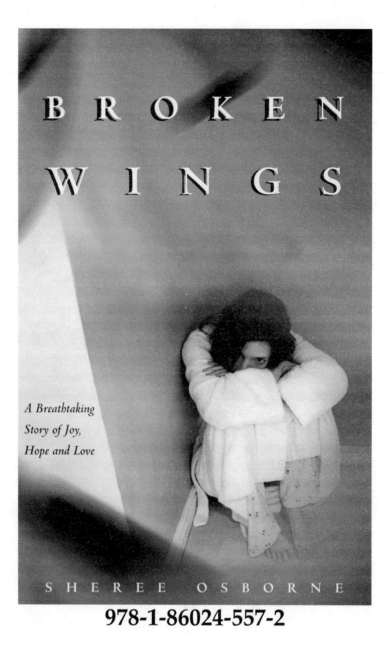

BROKEN WINGS

*A Breathtaking
Story of Joy,
Hope and Love*

SHEREE OSBORNE

978-1-86024-557-2